MINNESOTA SYMPOSIA ON
CHILD PSYCHOLOGY, VOLUME 3

MINNESOTA SYMPOSIA ON CHILD PSYCHOLOGY

Volume 3

JOHN P. HILL, EDITOR

THE UNIVERSITY OF MINNESOTA PRESS • MINNEAPOLIS

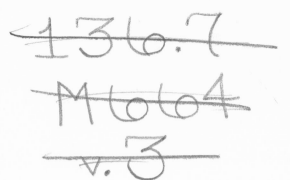

Library of Congress Catalog Card Number: 67-30520

PUBLISHED IN GREAT BRITAIN, INDIA, AND PAKISTAN BY THE OXFORD
UNIVERSITY PRESS, LONDON, BOMBAY, AND KARACHI, AND IN CANADA BY
THE COPP CLARK PUBLISHING CO. LIMITED, TORONTO

Preface

AT SOME point in the progress of a research program, the investigator usually is ready to call a moratorium on further empirical study — to spend some time reviewing the separate studies that compose the program so far, integrating new information with old, weighing the adequacy of the conceptual framework that has guided the program. Accepting an invitation to contribute to the Minnesota Symposia on Child Psychology can initiate such a moratorium or serve as an occasion for the formal termination of one already begun. In either case, the contribution provides focus for the investigator and for the reader. The investigator can use the process of preparation and the subsequent feedback to redirect his efforts; the reader can use the product to gain some insight into the particular investigator's overall frame of reference as well as into the area of specialization represented.

The distinguished investigators whose moratoria resulted in the papers of this volume were selected by faculty and graduate students of the Institute of Child Development. They presented their papers in 1968 at the third symposium in our annual series. The symposia and their publication are made possible by grants from the Public Health Service (National Institute of Child Health and Human Development HD-01765) and the Graduate School of the University of Minnesota. The editorial and production staffs of the University of Minnesota Press have aided authors and editor alike by their skill in shaping a book from six typescripts. The cooperation of all persons and organizations mentioned in this paragraph is gratefully acknowledged; the amiability with which it has been extended makes its acknowledgment especially gratifying.

The phenomena variously categorized under the concepts of stimulus change, novelty, incongruity, complexity, uncertainty, curiosity, exploration, and boredom have captured the interest of a large number of psychologists in the past decade. Among them is Gordon Cantor, whose program of research on stimulus familiarization is reported here. A Stimulus Familiarization Effect (SFE) is demonstrated to occur in a series of studies. Children respond more quickly to a nonfamiliarized than to a familiarized stimulus. When placed in control of a projection device, they also tend to project a nonfamiliarized stimulus for longer durations than they do a familiarized one. In addition, studies involving the rating of stimuli on a like-dislike scale show that children prefer nonfamiliarized stimuli. Cantor discusses the implications of SFE in terms of heightened drive level owing to the introduction of a "surprising" nonfamiliar stimulus; interference with responding to the familiarized stimulus owing to the build-up of competing attending responses; and the habituation of the orientation reaction to the familiarized stimulus. Cantor thinks that the latter argument better explains SFE but is aware of the vagaries implicit in the concept of orientation reaction. The reader is led to ask, with Cantor, what boredom is that we be mindful of it.

Attentional processes are the focus of two other papers in this volume as well: Jeffrey on "Early Stimulation and Cognitive Development" and Maccoby on "The Development of Stimulus Selection." As does Cantor, Jeffrey finds in the habituation concept potential for explaining effects of varying regimens of exposure to stimuli. Jeffrey's immediate purposes are rather more developmental, however, and he proposes a serial habituation model to account for the relatively passive exploratory behavior of the infant. The model then is applied to some aspects of the development of object perception, abstractions, and conservation. Jeffrey sets his work within the context of current reaction to Behaviorism, presenting one variant of the sometimes direct and sometimes subtle conflict between centralism and peripheralism that characterizes contemporary psychology and that is reflected in many of the papers in this series.

Maccoby takes as her problem the developmental understanding of the selective processes operative when children are asked to select a subpart of a complex of stimuli. She derives several hypotheses about the development of stimulus selection which integrate data from her own program of research on dichotic listening. Increasing age is accompanied by more efficient orientation of the sense organs, but the older child's increased ability to perceive selectively also is a function of more central events: "With increasing age, the child's perceptions are more and more dominated by organized search patterns that are related to sustained 'plans' or ongoing behavior patterns of the perceiver" (p. 94). That the hypotheses Maccoby generates are germane to a number of live issues in the psychologies of attention and development may be seen in her discussions of the match between her formulations and those of Broadbent, Neisser, Piaget, and Werner.

The derivation and articulation of some useful generalizations from a body of research is also the tack taken by Denenberg in his paper. He reports on the implications for human development of animal studies of early experience. Early experience, of many different kinds and degrees, is shown to effect dramatic changes in characteristics that some versions of common sense would hold to be the least amenable to modification— namely, those which have a strong genetic base and those which have high survival value. Denenberg illustrates, as well, some of the multiple effects and long-term consequences which early experiences can cause, depending upon the age at which they occur. The profound modification by early experience of important behavior systems in animals leads Denenberg to the conviction that in the first two years of life the human infant is especially vulnerable to the opportunities and limitations of his environment.

Denenberg thus provides further sanction, if any is needed, for the current interest of developmental psychologists in infancy. While the population of infant studies is exploding, that of adolescent studies remains on a low plateau. This is unfortunate, for, as Muzafer and Carolyn Sherif point out, the universal changes in the biochemistry and structure of the body and the changes in social expectations which set off the adolescent period have important developmental sequelae. The Sherifs' own work has to do with the structure and functions of natural reference groups during adolescence. Much of our basic knowledge of the differences and similarities between reference groups and their effects at various social class levels and in varying sociocultural settings comes from the Sherifs' continuing program of research on this topic. The distinctive combination of field and experimental strategies and of social and individual concepts that characterizes their work is well illustrated in discussions of goals, status, and conformity in the adolescent reference group.

As interaction with members of reference groups shapes and provides potent models for social behavior, so does interaction with parents and siblings. The ways in which such interactions and their effects differ depending upon birth order have been problems of interest to psychologists of many different persuasions. Most of the empirical expressions of this interest have suffered from inadequate controls (e.g., for maternal age, for socioeconomic status, for family size) and from ignoring sex of siblings, spacing of siblings, and specific ordinal positions (e.g., as occurs in comparisons of firstborn versus all later children). The research reported here by Sutton-Smith and Rosenberg was designed with the elimination of these limitations in mind. As a result, an important new data base has emerged from their extensive series of studies. The examination of the entire family constellation and the reciprocal relationships within it that is required to render birth-order studies interpretable necessarily complicates conclusions about first- and later borns. There appears to be promise for extracting some meaningful generalizations from birth-order data in Sutton-Smith and Rosenberg's distinction between effects that are the outcome of reactions to others in the family constellation and those that are the outcome of modeling upon them. Reaction and modeling both are components of sibling and parent-child interaction. The authors advocate the direct and molecular study of such interaction as a way out of the morass of inferences typically involved in explaining the chain of events that links birth order to its outcomes.

The papers in this volume, like those in the preceding volumes, demonstrate the vigor and variety of contemporary developmental research. The Institute of Child Development is pleased to be able to share them with colleagues in psychology and others interested in the development and behavior of children.

JOHN P. HILL

Minneapolis, Minnesota
August 1969

Table of Contents

MINNESOTA SYMPOSIA ON CHILD PSYCHOLOGY, VOLUME 3

◈ GORDON N. CANTOR ◈

Effects of Stimulus Familiarization on Child Behavior

FOR many years now, behavior scientists identified in one way or another with the area of child development have argued about how one decides whether a given piece of behavioral research does or does not constitute a developmental study. Were the members of the Society for Research in Child Development or of Division 7 of the American Psychological Association to be polled on this matter, I think there is little doubt that the single most frequently cited criterion would involve the question of whether or not the investigator included chronological age (CA) as an independent variable in his research. Such a reaction would be predicated, I believe, on the generally agreed upon premise that those laws we categorize as developmental in nature serve to relate variations in behavior to variations in CA. But, as developmentalists, do we tend to be satisfied with the discovery of such laws, no matter how useful they may be in practice? I think not. We wish to know *why* the changes pinpointed by developmental laws occur. Such considerations carry us beyond simple statements regarding CA-behavior relations to attempts at discovering the *mechanisms* or *processes* involved. In this search for mechanisms, the developmentalist accustomed to varying CA as an independent variable in his research may choose at some juncture in his career to perform a series of studies in which children at one given age level serve as subjects. I consider it unreasonable to contend that such a shift in emphasis or strategy transforms a developmentalist into a non-developmentalist.

NOTE: I am indebted to William L. Croll for his constructive critical comments on this paper.

3

In his discussion of this topic at the conference commemorating the fortieth anniversary of the Institute of Child Development at the University of Minnesota, Charles Spiker (1966) took the position that CA need not *necessarily* be an independent variable in a study in order for that investigation to contribute to our understanding of developmental phenomena. By way of illustration, he suggested that, knowing that five-year-olds condition quickly and two-year-olds condition not at all in a particular learning situation, one might study the conditioning behavior of five-year-olds in order to arrive at an understanding of the variables affecting performance of children at that age. Armed with such knowledge, his argument continues, one might then be in a position to understand why two-year-olds do not normally learn in such a situation and, possibly, how to arrange conditions so that they do.

Another way of supporting Spiker's position, it seems to me, is to argue that doing research with children of a given age may have important developmental implications if the task used by the investigator in some way telescopes an experiential phenomenon that occurs across time in the ordinary life circumstances of the developing child. I should like to submit that the study of the stimulus familiarization variable provides as good an illustration of this sort of approach as one might imagine. Whatever else the developing infant and child may be experiencing, assuming no severe atypicality in his psychobiological makeup or in his environment, surely he is continually being introduced to and becoming familiar with untold numbers and varieties of stimuli in his environment. The administration of a stimulus familiarization treatment to children of a given age in the laboratory amounts, in my view, to a controlled, miniature version of a ubiquitous phenomenon which occurs and reoccurs with regularity as time passes in the everyday life of the developing child.

Though one might grant that the stimulus familiarization experiment may have developmental implications, he may nevertheless question the psychological significance of the familiarization variable, under the assumption that not all developmental changes are necessarily psychologically interesting or significant. Does it matter, psychologically, that familiarization events do constitute a part of the developing organism's experience? For a period of some fifteen years, several behavior scientists have indicated in various ways — at least with respect to animal behavior — that they think it does matter (e.g., Berlyne, 1960; Butler, 1953; Dember,

4

1961; Fowler, 1967; Glanzer, 1953; Harlow, 1953; Myers & Miller, 1954; Montgomery, 1954).

Viewed from a broad perspective, many of the writers concerned with this topic may be designated, using the terminology of O'Connell (1965), as either "tedium" or "titillation" theorists. "Tedium" theorists (e.g., Glanzer, 1953; Myers & Miller, 1954) emphasize the consequences of continued exposure to an unchanging stimulus surround. The common sense notion of boredom comes immediately to mind when one examines this type of formulation. The "titillation" theorists (e.g., Harlow, 1953; Montgomery, 1954), in contrast, stress the role played by what Berlyne (1960) has called the "collative" variables — that is, stimulus change, novelty, incongruity, complexity, uncertainty, and so forth.

Each of these approaches has its difficulties. The "tedium" emphases suffer mainly from incompleteness, since they ignore the role played by the collative variables. The "titillation" formulations, while recognizing the importance of the collative variables, ignore the boredom variable and suffer from other, more vexing problems. For example, exposure to a novel stimulus is said by some to increase the so-called "exploratory drive," while continued commerce with the same stimulus is said to lead eventually to drive reduction. Such an approach has led certain theorists to attribute reinforcing properties to drive induction as well as drive reduction (Montgomery, 1954), or to use an "optimal level of stimulation" conceptualization (Leuba, 1955), or to invent an ingenious but rather tortuously labored formulation regarding the role of the collative variables in producing a state of conflict in the organism (Berlyne, 1960). In some of the best-known animal work in the area, Butler (1953) has reported that monkeys enclosed within a box will learn to solve a discrimination task and will continue to respond for extended periods to obtain a view of the environment outside the box. On the basis of such findings, a form of "titillation" theory is employed which invokes the concept of a "visual-exploration" drive. But, as Judson Brown has pointed out (1961, pp. 336–337):

That this view leads to difficulties should be clear from the following: If the act of looking out of the windows at the outside (laboratory) world is the specific event that arouses the visual-exploration drive, then the monkeys do not have this drive until they have succeeded in opening the correct window. The drive aroused by the final act of visual exploration cannot, therefore, provide the impetus for the response of window opening. External stimuli, when seen, may indeed incite a drive to explore with the

5

eyes, but it is illogical to say that those stimuli, *while they are invisible to the monkey,* actively function to arouse the drive to work in order to see.*

A recent and, in my opinion, very significant formulation proposed by Fowler (1967) combines the "tedium" with the "titillation" approach, while avoiding the pitfalls of earlier "titillation" theories. In brief, Fowler assumes that continued exposure to an unchanging stimulus surround produces a drive ("boredom") state in the organism. This, of course, is the "tedium" aspect of the theory. The "titillation" emphasis is dealt with through Fowler's assumption that stimulus change can serve as an incentive for the organism. It is apparent that Fowler's approach involves a transformation of the Hull-Spence drive-incentive formulation (as applied, for example, to the behavior of a hungry rat running in a runway for food reward) so as to make that theoretical schema applicable to so-called exploratory behavior. The relevance of Fowler's formulation to some of the child familiarization data with which we shall deal will be given consideration below.

The child familiarization studies to be discussed here fall into three major classes. The first group is concerned with the speed of children's motor responses to familiarized and nonfamiliarized stimuli. As we shall see, the data in question are not amenable to easy theoretical analysis. In fact, none of the approaches mentioned thus far appears to be applicable, and I shall find it necessary to use certain concepts — namely, the "orientation reaction" (OR) (Lynn, 1966) and "habituation" (Thompson & Spencer, 1966) — not commonly employed in the theorizing of American workers interested in so-called exploratory or curiosity behaviors. The second major group of experiments is concerned with the relative amounts of time children spend projecting familiarized and nonfamiliarized visual stimuli. The third major category includes recently collected data concerning children's like-dislike ratings of familiarized and nonfamiliarized visual stimuli and children's behavior in situations in which they are forced to attend to repetitive, unchanging, uninteresting visual stimulation. It will be argued that a substantial part of the data falling in the latter two major categories is at least consistent with a formulation such as that proposed by Fowler, whereas one segment of the results is in definite conflict with the theory.

* From *The Motivation of Behavior* by Judson Brown. Copyright 1961 by Mc-Graw-Hill. Used by permission of McGraw-Hill Book Company.

Speed of Children's Responses to Familiarized and Nonfamiliarized Stimuli

We are concerned here with what has come to be termed the "stimulus familiarization effect" (SFE) (Bogartz & Witte, 1966). The effect has now been demonstrated in a total of ten child studies performed in the Iowa laboratories; I shall examine here the eight studies listed in the summary on pages 8–9 (see also Bogartz & Witte, 1966, Exp. II; Witte, 1965). The basic experimental paradigm for the SFE studies includes the following features. First, the subject is exposed to a series of familiarization trials involving one of two stimuli. (With the exception of one experiment, in which a light and a buzzer were employed, all of the studies I shall consider included use of a red and a green light as stimuli.) A counterbalancing procedure is used so that half the subjects are familiarized on one stimulus, and the remaining subjects on the second stimulus. Following familiarization, the subject is given a series of trials on a motor task in which the previously familiarized stimulus serves as the signal to respond on half the trials, the nonfamiliarized stimulus serving this function on the remaining trials. Typically, the sequential occurrences of the two stimuli are determined semi-randomly, with equal numbers of presentations of the two signals taking place within successive blocks of trials.

Variations on this procedural theme characterize certain of the experiments; I shall note these special features as seems appropriate. The major procedural details, as well as the results of the studies to be discussed, are summarized on pages 8–9. The SFE is said to have been demonstrated when, on the average, the subjects respond significantly faster to the nonfamiliarized than to the familiarized stimulus in the motor task.

In the initial study in this series (G. N. Cantor & J. H. Cantor, 1964), children of kindergarten age were exposed to forty two-second presentations of either a light or buzzer stimulus. Subsequently, the subject responded on a series of lever-pulling trials, the familiarized and the nonfamiliarized stimulus each serving as the signal to respond on half the trials. Two measures were obtained for each lever-pulling trial: (a) starting time (the time from stimulus onset until the subject moved his hand from a start position and pulled the lever down a fraction of an inch); and (b) movement time (the time taken to move the lever through the remainder of its 15-inch excursion). These values were reciprocalized to produce speed scores.

Table 1 shows the mean *starting* speeds for the two stimuli across trial

Summary of the Studies of Stimulus Familiarization Effect (SFE)

	Nondifferential Responding				Differential Responding			
	G. N. Cantor & J. H. Cantor, 1964	Witte, 1967	Witte & Cantor, 1967	Bogartz & Witte, 1966, Exp. I	G. N. Cantor & J. H. Cantor, 1965	G. N. Cantor & J. H. Cantor, 1966	Miller, 1966	G. N. Cantor & Fenson, 1968
Task	lever pulling	lever pulling	lever pulling	finger withdrawal	button pressing	button pressing	button release & pressing	button release & pressing
Subjects	60 kindergartners	28 4- to 5-year-olds	40 5- to 6-year-olds	20 kindergartners	40 (mean CA 5 yr. 1 mo.)	80 4- to 6-year-olds	160 first-graders	120 kindergartners
Motor task stimuli[a]	W light & buzzer	R & G lights	R & G lights	R & G lights	R & G lights	R & G lights	R & G lights	R & G lights
No. of familiarization trials & stimuli involved[a]	40 (light or buzzer)	40 (20R & 20G; 4.5 vs. 1.5 sec.)	20 (R or G)	20 (R or G)	40 (R or G)	40 (35R, 5W; 5R, 35W; 35G, 5W; 5G, 35W)	40 (0, 1, 10, 20, or 40 R or G+40, 39, 30, 20, or 0 W)	18 (5, 10, 12, 14, 16, or 18 R or G+13, 8, 6, 4, 2, or 0 W)
Stimulus duration in familiarization phase	2 sec.	1.5 or 4.5 sec.	4 sec.	depended on S's response speed	3 sec.	3 sec.	3 sec.	3 sec.

8

Motor response in familiarization phase	no	no	no	yes	no	no	no	no
No. of motor task trials; stimuli involved[a]	48 (24 light, 24 buzzer)	24 (12 R, 12 G)	32 (16 R, 16 G)	30 (15 R, 15 G)	50 (25 R, 25 G)	48 (24 R, 24 G)	48 (24 R, 24 G)	48 (24 R, 24 G)
Response to stimulus in motor task	onset	onset	offset	onset	onset	onset	onset	onset
Measure(s) in motor task and obtained SFE[b]	SS, yes; MS, no	SS, yes; MS, no	SS, yes; MS, yes	RS, yes	response speed, yes	response speed, yes	RS, yes (for 20 & 40 familiarization trials); TS, no	RS, yes (for 18 familiarization trials); TS, no
SFE durability	no sig. decrease across trial blocks	sig. for trial block 1 but not for 2	no sig. decrease across trial blocks	trials variable not included in analysis	no sig. decrease across trial blocks	crossover on third of 3 trial blocks	no sig. decrease across trial blocks	sig. for trial block 1 but not for 2

[a] R = red, G = green, W = white.
[b] SS = starting speed, MS = movement speed, RS = release speed, TS = travel speed.

Table 1. Mean Starting Speeds to the Nonfamiliar and Familiar Stimulus
(Buzzer and Light Combined) across Three-Trial Blocks

Stimulus	Trial Block								Overall
	1	2	3	4	5	6	7	8	
Nonfamiliar .	.998	1.093	1.030	.997	1.004	1.003	1.016	1.018	1.020
Familiar	.960	1.024	1.009	.987	.978	.978	.961	.988	.986

SOURCE: G. N. Cantor & J. H. Cantor, 1964.

blocks. As is evident in this table, the subjects responded more quickly to the nonfamiliarized stimulus; the familiarity effect was statistically significant. Two other significant effects were obtained — that for sense modality (surprisingly, speeds were faster in response to the light than to the buzzer) and that for trial blocks. The latter effect was doubtless produced by the sharp rise in speeds to both stimuli on trial block 2; this particular pattern of speed changes occurring across trials has never been replicated in subsequently gathered data and probably should not be taken seriously. The interaction between the familiarity and the sense modality variable was not significant, indicating that a comparable SFE was obtained when the light and when the buzzer served as the familiarized stimulus. The magnitude of the SFE did not change significantly across trial blocks. Analysis of the *movement* speed data failed to reveal any significant effects, except in the case of the trial blocks variable.

In a second lever study, with five- and six-year-olds, Witte (1967) departed from the usual SFE paradigm by presenting *both* stimuli — a red and a green light in this case — *during familiarization.* One stimulus was presented twenty times for four and a half seconds, the other twenty times for one and a half seconds, with the appropriate counterbalancing included. In the subsequently administered lever task, the subjects responded with significantly faster *starting* speeds to the stimulus familiarized at the 1.5-second duration. The relevant mean starting speeds across six-trial blocks (from Witte, 1967) are:

Stimulus	Trial Block 1	Trial Block 2	Overall
High familiar	.90	.86	.88
Low familiar	.98	.87	.92

One has evidence here for the SFE when speeds of responding to stimuli differing in *extent of prior exposure* (rather than to a familiarized and a nonfamiliarized stimulus) are compared. In this case, the SFE did dissipate across trials, the effect being nonsignificant for the latter half of the motor task trials. Again, the *movement* speed analysis revealed no evidence for the occurrence of the SFE.

In the final lever study to be discussed here (Witte & Cantor, 1967), five- and six-year-olds observed twenty 4-second presentations of a red or of a green light. The subsequently administered motor task, entailing sixteen presentations of each stimulus, differed from those of the earlier studies in that the subject was instructed to respond to the *offset* rather than the onset of the stimuli. On each lever-pulling trial, the stimulus remained on for 4 seconds, the subject being instructed to keep his hand on a start mark until offset of the light. A significant SFE was obtained in the case of *both* the starting and movement speed measure in this experiment. The relevant start speed means are .92 and .94 for the familiar and the nonfamiliar stimulus, respectively; the movement speed means are 3.07 and 3.15 for the familiar and the nonfamiliar stimulus, respectively. There was no evidence for dissipation of the SFE across trials in the case of either response measure.

In the experiment to be considered next, Bogartz and Witte (1966, Exp. I) gave children of kindergarten age fifty simple reaction time (RT) trials. The task entailed finger withdrawal from a button at the onset of a colored light stimulus. For the first twenty trials, a given subject was exposed to only one color of light — red or green; this constituted the familiarization phase. During the remaining thirty trials, the familiarized and the nonfamiliarized light each served as the signal to respond half the time. Note that, in contrast to all the other SFE studies on pages 8–9, motor responses were required here in the familiarization as well as in the test phase. The implications of this fact will be considered below. Analysis of the response speed data for the test phase indicated that responses were significantly faster to the nonfamiliarized than to the familiarized stimulus — that is, the usual SFE was obtained.

I turn now to a series of four studies employing choice RT as the motor task. In the first of these (G. N. Cantor & J. H. Cantor, 1965), children of preschool age were presented forty three-second exposures of a red or a green light. A choice RT task was then administered, each of the two stimuli serving as the signal to respond on half of fifty RT trials. The subject was instructed to move his hand from a start position at the onset of a stimulus, pressing a red button in response to the red light and a green button in response to the green light. Response speeds to the nonfamiliarized light were significantly faster than those to the familiarized light. Table 2 shows the means of interest here. Note that the SFE appears not to have been present on trial block 1, but was obtained for the remaining trial blocks. The interaction of the familiarization and trial block variables was not statistically significant, however.

Table 2. Mean Response Speeds to the Nonfamiliar and
Familiar Stimulus (Red and Green Combined)
across Five-Trial Blocks

Stimulus	Trial Block					
	1	2	3	4	5	Overall
Nonfamiliar	.892	.904	.815	.780	.771	.832
Familiar	.888	.851	.780	.743	.758	.804

SOURCE: G. N. Cantor & J. H. Cantor, 1965.

A second choice RT study (G. N. Cantor & J. H. Cantor, 1966) was similar to that just described, except that the amount of familiarization was varied. Forty three-second stimulus exposures were given to the four-through six-year-olds serving as subjects in this experiment. Amount of familiarization was varied by including either thirty-five or five exposures to a light of a given color (red or green). Additional presentations (five or thirty-five) of a white light served to equate the total number of exposures given. Following familiarization, forty-eight choice RT trials were administered, the red and the green light each serving as the signal to respond on half the trials. The white light played no role in the motor task phase. Speeds were significantly faster in response to the nonfamiliarized than to the familiarized stimulus. The pertinent means are presented in Table 3. In contrast to the finding in the earlier choice RT study (G. N. Cantor & J. H. Cantor, 1965), the SFE in this case did dissipate over trials, the overall speeds to the nonfamiliarized stimulus being substantially faster than those to the familiarized stimulus over the first two thirds, but slightly slower over the final third of the trials. Most unexpected was the failure of the amount-of-familiarization variable to interact significantly with the familiarized versus nonfamiliarized variable. Taken at face value, this finding indicates that SFE's of comparable magnitude can be produced using five and thirty-five stimulus familiarization exposures.

Skepticism regarding the replicability of the finding just discussed led Frank Miller, in his doctoral dissertation (1966), to investigate the SFE

Table 3. Mean Response Speeds to the Nonfamiliar and
Familiar Stimulus (Red and Green Combined)
across Eight-Trial Blocks

Group and Stimulus	Trial Block			
	1	2	3	Overall
Low amount				
Nonfamiliar	.982	.931	.889	.934
Familiar	.964	.908	.884	.919
High amount				
Nonfamiliar	.977	.920	.868	.922
Familiar	.940	.876	.886	.901
All subjects				
Nonfamiliar	.980	.925	.879	.928
Familiar	.952	.892	.885	.910

SOURCE: G. N. Cantor & J. H. Cantor, 1966.

using 0, 1, 10, 20, and 40 presentations of the familiarization stimulus. As in the previous study, additional exposures of a white light were used to equate the groups for total number of familiarization trials. The subjects were first-graders. In his choice RT task, Miller included a third button as a start position, thus enabling him to obtain two measures — release speed (the reciprocal of the time taken to release the start button following stimulus onset) and travel speed (the reciprocal of the time intervening between start button release and pressing of the appropriate response button). Table 4 shows the overall mean *release* speeds to the two stimuli for the five amount-of-familiarization groups. As an examination of this table suggests, there was a significant interaction between the amount and familiarized versus nonfamiliarized stimulus variables. Table 4 also shows the mean release speeds across trial blocks for the groups given 0, 1, 10, 20, and 40 familiarization exposures. Although there was a tendency for speeds to be faster in response to the nonfamiliarized stimulus in Groups 1 and 10, none of the main effects of the familiarization variable was significant in Groups 0, 1, and 10. For Groups 20 and 40, in contrast, release speeds were significantly faster in response to the nonfamiliarized than to the familiarized stimulus. When the data for these two groups were combined in an overall analysis, no significant interaction between the amount and familiarized versus nonfamiliarized variables was revealed, indicating that a comparable SFE was obtained for twenty and forty familiarization exposures. No indication that the SFE dissipated across trials was evident in the performance of Groups 20 and 40. With regard to

Table 4. Mean Release Speeds to the Nonfamiliar and
Familiar Stimulus (Red and Green Combined)
across Eight-Trial Blocks for Groups
0, 1, 10, 20, and 40

	Trial Block			
Stimulus	1	2	3	Overall
Group 0[a]				
Nonfamiliar	1.657	1.519	1.501	1.559
Familiar	1.659	1.539	1.500	1.566
Group 1				
Nonfamiliar	1.784	1.627	1.569	1.660
Familiar	1.749	1.591	1.520	1.620
Group 10				
Nonfamiliar	1.804	1.739	1.649	1.730
Familiar	1.829	1.684	1.616	1.710
Group 20				
Nonfamiliar	1.733	1.675	1.551	1.653
Familiar	1.657	1.552	1.465	1.558
Group 40				
Nonfamiliar	1.699	1.648	1.596	1.648
Familiar	1.644	1.514	1.458	1.539

SOURCE: From Miller, 1966, p. 49. Reproduced here by
permission of the author.
[a] Arbitrary stimulus designations via random assignment
for Group 0.

the *travel* speed data, no evidence for the occurrence of the SFE was revealed.

The final SFE study (G. N. Cantor & Fenson, 1968) to be discussed here was designed to resolve the question of whether or not the SFE is obtainable using fewer than 20 familiarization trials. This experiment, involving subjects of kindergarten age, essentially replicated the Miller (1966) procedures. The following numbers of red or green light familiarization trials were employed: 5, 10, 12, 14, 16, and 18. Again, presentations of a white light were given to equate the groups for total number of familiarization exposures. Evidence for the SFE in the choice RT task was obtained only in the starting speed data for the group given 18 familiarization trials. This effect was present only in the first half of the motor task trials. Again, no SFE was evident in the travel speed data.

On the basis of the results obtained in Cantor and Fenson's study, as well as in Miller's experiment, it seems reasonable to conclude that the earlier finding of the SFE following only five familiarization exposures (G. N. Cantor & J. H. Cantor, 1966) is probably not replicable.

THEORETICAL ANALYSIS OF THE SFE DATA

Two potential explanations of the SFE come readily to mind, but can as readily be shown to be inappropriate. First, there is the possibility that the occurrence of the nonfamiliarized stimulus in the motor task "surprises" the subject, leading to a temporary increase in drive level and hence increased speed of responding. One must immediately wonder, in this context, why there was so little evidence for the SFE in the travel or movement speed components of the various motor responses. As indicated under "obtained SFE" on page 9, of the five studies which included a breakdown of the response measure into two components, all five revealed the SFE for the "initiation" component, but only one revealed it for the "execution" component. It would seem that heightened drive owing to surprise should be as facilitating for execution as for initiation responses. A second consideration making the surprise hypothesis suspect has to do with the relative durability of the SFE. Of the seven studies summarized on pages 8–9 providing for trials analysis, four showed no significant change in the SFE across trial blocks (see SFE durability). It does not seem plausible to argue that the occurrence of the nonfamiliarized stimulus was "surprising" and continued to remain so over a considerable number of trials. Finally, the surprise hypothesis would be difficult to reconcile with the fact that the SFE was obtained by Witte (1967) when *both* stimuli were presented in the familiarization phase (one for four and a half and one for one and a half seconds).

A second possible interpretation of the SFE, making use of an associative interference notion, suggests that perhaps the child acquires a tendency during the familiarization phase to make prolonged attending responses to the familiarized stimulus — such responses then persisting in the motor task so as to interfere with prompt responding. Evidence inconsistent with this hypothesis is contained in the study by Bogartz and Witte (1966, Exp. I), in which the subjects performed a motor response in the *familiarization* as well as in the motor task phase. There would be no reason to expect competing attending responses to have been built up during a familiarization phase of this sort. In fact, one might expect the test phase response speeds in this case to have been faster to the *familiarized* stimulus, as a result of the practice the subjects received in making the motor response to this stimulus during the familiarization phase. But this was not the case — the usual SFE was obtained. The associative interference interpretation also fails to fare well in light of the finding by Witte and Cantor (1967) that the SFE is obtainable when the subjects are instructed to respond to stimulus *offset* in the motor task situation. It is difficult to see how prolonged attending responses, assuming they were developed in the familiarization phase, could have had an interfering effect at the time of stimulus offset on a given motor task trial.

A third possible explanation of the SFE is suggested by the previously noted tendency for the effect to occur in the initiation but not in the execution or movement component of the motor response. What may be implicated here is an attentional mechanism quite different from that previously discussed — a mechanism which involves habituation of the "orientation reaction" (OR).

Application of OR and habituation theorizing to the SFE would appear to require the following series of arguments. First, it is assumed that the initial occurrences of the stimulus in the familiarization phase elicit the OR. With repeated presentations (apparently on the order of 18 or more), the OR habituates to that stimulus. Next, it is assumed that, at the onset of the motor task, *both* stimuli would be invested with "signal" character and hence here should elicit roughly comparable OR's. However, as the motor task trials progress, rehabituation of the OR to the familiarized stimulus should occur relatively rapidly (because of the prior habituation occurring in the familiarization phase), whereas OR habituation to the nonfamiliarized stimulus should occur more slowly (because of its relatively nonfamiliar character). Finally, it is assumed that speed of responding in the motor task is in general positively related to the strength and the reliability of occurrence of the OR, the SFE reflecting the differentially strong OR's elicited by the two stimuli in question.

I approach this explanation of the SFE with misgivings, for at present it can be formulated in only a vague and speculative manner. The concept of *habituation*, as recently discussed by Thompson and Spencer (1966), strikes me as a relatively clear one, having well-documented behavioral manifestations. In contrast, however, the OR concept, referring to a bewildering complex of events (such as changes in sense organ sensitivity, occurrence of receptor orienting responses, changes in skeletal musculature, and changes in EEG and several vegetative processes), cannot in my opinion be regarded as a very clear one. As Wickens (1967, pp. 114–115) has noted, "Our knowledge of the relationship between these kinds of responses tells us . . . they are far from perfectly correlated . . .

Since the various measures of the *OR* are far from perfectly correlated, which measures should be used to predict its occurrence?"

Considering this criticism of OR theorizing (and others as well) as valid, I can hardly defend the OR habituation explanation of the SFE with enthusiasm. But I am aware of no explanation having more or even as much potential. Drawing on the writings of persons such as Sokolov (1963; 1965), Lynn (1966), and Maltzman (Maltzman, 1967; Maltzman & Raskin, 1965; Maltzman, Raskin, Johnson, & Gould, 1965), and examining the SFE data available to us at present, I can only make the following assertions: (a) the OR, defined in various ways, does appear to undergo a habituation process owing to repeated stimulus presentations; (b) the magnitude of the OR (again, defined in various ways) does appear to affect performance in a variety of situations, including speed of responding in motor tasks; (c) in at least some of our SFE data (see, e.g., Table 2), there is no noticeable SFE in the initial motor task trials, as theorizing regarding OR habituation and the role played by so-called "signal" stimuli would demand; and, finally, (d) the prolonged pattern in the SFE studies of faster responding to the nonfamiliarized stimulus, following the initial motor task trials, is at least *consistent* with the OR-habituation point of view.

What is badly needed is a series of studies combining administration of the SFE paradigm with use of various of the measures assumed to compose the OR. Unfortunately, the one completed study of which I am aware that used this approach — a study by Meyers and Joseph (1968) employing GSR measurement and adults as subjects — failed to demonstrate a significant SFE, probably owing to the use of an insufficient number of stimulus familiarization trials.

Children's Projections of Familiarized and Nonfamiliarized Stimuli

I turn now to a series of three studies designed to determine if children, when put in control of a projection device, will project familiarized and nonfamiliarized stimuli for different time durations.

In the first of these experiments (J. H. Cantor & G. N. Cantor, 1964b), twenty pictures selected from the Welsh Figure Preference Test (Welsh, 1959) were used. These are shown in Figure 1. The upper ten stimuli in the figure composed set A, the lower ten set B.

For half of sixty-six subjects of kindergarten age, the pictures in set A served as familiarization stimuli. The child sat and observed the auto-

Figure 1. Welsh Figure Preference Test stimuli used in Cantor & Cantor, 1964b. The figures numbered 1–10 composed Set A, 11–20 Set B. Reproduced by special permission from George S. Welsh, *Welsh Figure Preference Test* (Palo Alto, Calif.: Consulting Psychologists Press, copyright 1949).

matic presentation of each of the ten stimuli (six seconds on, two seconds off) across five blocks of presentations, a different random order of appearance of the ten stimuli being used in each block. The remaining subjects were familiarized in comparable fashion with the stimuli of set B. Following the fifty exposures (five per stimulus), the subject was taught to control the stimulus projections himself by pushing a spring-mounted rod. The subject then ran through two additional blocks of projections of the familiarization stimuli, the duration of exposure in each case being recorded by the experimenter.

Half the children were then given a five-minute rest, following which they resumed the projection activity. In this (test) phase, the subject projected each of the ten familiarized stimuli and each of the ten previously unseen stimuli once apiece. The stimulus sequence was such that one stimulus from each set occurred within a block of two projections, the order of appearance of the familiarized and the nonfamiliarized stimulus within a block being randomly determined. Again the experimenter recorded the length of exposure of each stimulus. The remaining subjects were treated identically, except that a two-day rather than a five-minute period intervened between the familiarization and the test phase.

The test phase time scores were reciprocalized in order to obtain more nearly normally distributed data. Hence, a numerically high score in this context is associated with relatively *short* exposure durations. The graphs contained in Figure 2 present the results of interest here. The top two graphs deal with the projections of the children given the five-minute (S, for *short*) interval between familiarization and testing; the middle pair of graphs presents the results for the subjects who returned to the test phase after a two-day (L, for *long*) interval. The left-hand graphs in both rows pertain to the subjects familiarized on set A (Groups SA and LA), the right-hand graphs to those familiarized on set B (Groups SB and LB). Note that the data have been organized into two-trial blocks.

Examination of these four graphs reveals that: (a) in each case, projections of the nonfamiliarized stimuli tended to be longer than those of the familiarized stimuli; and (b) the overall projection durations were shorter for Group SA than for the remaining three groups. The latter relation is illustrated in the bottom right-hand graph, where the data are collapsed over the familiarization variable. The assumption that a difference in sampling probably is involved here was considered and is given support by the finding that the subjects in Group SA also projected stimuli

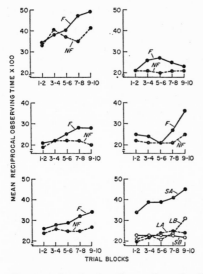

Figure 2. Mean reciprocal projection times (× 100) plotted across two-trial blocks (J. H. Cantor & G. N. Cantor, 1964b). The letter codes have the following meanings: (a) F = familiar, NF = nonfamiliar; (b) A = stimulus Set A familiar, B = stimulus Set B familiar; (c) S = short interval between familiarization and testing, L = long interval between familiarization and testing. The top two graphs present the data for the subgroups tested following the short interval, and the middle two graphs the data for the subgroups tested following the long interval; in each case, the left-hand graph is for the group familiarized on stimulus Set A, the right-hand graph for the group familiarized on stimulus Set B. The bottom left graph presents the overall means for the familiar and nonfamiliar stimuli, collapsed over the counterbalancing subgroups. The bottom right graph presents the means for the four counterbalancing subgroups, collapsed over the familiar-nonfamiliar variable. Reproduced by permission from *Child Development*, 1964, 35, 124.

for relatively short durations during the final two projection series of the familiarization phase.

The finding of central interest, of course, lies in the tendency for all four groups to project the nonfamiliarized stimuli for longer durations. The bottom left-hand graph in Figure 2 presents the overall means of concern here. In an analysis of variance applied to these data, the main effect for the familiarity variable proved to be significant at well beyond the .01 level. Completely unexpected was the failure to obtain an interaction between the familiarity variable and the length of the interval separating the familiarization from the test phase. That is, the pattern of findings represented in the bottom left-hand graph held regardless of whether testing occurred five minutes or two days following the familiarization exposures.

In the second projection study (J. H. Cantor & G. N. Cantor, 1964a), which also involved kindergarten children as subjects, color cartoon materials were used as stimuli. The design was essentially like that of the study just described, with the exception that *amount of familiarization* was introduced as an additional independent variable. Half the subjects were given eight exposures of each of ten familiarization stimuli, whereas the remaining subjects received only two. Additional exposures to stimuli irrelevant to the test phase were given to the latter subjects in order to equate for total number of stimulus exposure trials occurring in the familiarization phase. The results are summarized in Table 5. Again, note that numerically high means signify short exposure durations.

Table 5. Means of Reciprocal Observing Time (1/sec.)
across Five-Trial Blocks with Short and Long
Delay between Familiarization and Test

	Delay		
Stimulus	Short	Long	Overall
Two familiarization exposures			
Nonfamiliar	.205	.221	.213
Familiar	.235	.239	.237
Eight familiarization exposures			
Nonfamiliar	.219	.235	.227
Familiar	.287	.306	.296

SOURCE: J. H. Cantor & G. N. Cantor, 1964a.

Again, projections of the nonfamiliarized stimuli were longer than those of the familiarized stimuli, with the differences being significantly greater for the subjects given the larger as opposed to the smaller number of familiarization exposures. It should be emphasized, however, that the familiarization effect was statistically significant for *both* amount-of-familiarization groups. Once again, the period of delay between familiarization and testing did not interact with the familiarity variable — that is, the differences between exposure durations for familiarized and nonfamiliarized stimuli were comparable when a five-minute and a two-day interval intervened between familiarization and testing.

In the final projection study (J. H. Cantor & G. N. Cantor, 1966), one hundred and eight kindergarten children served as subjects. Drawings from the Welsh Figure Preference Test were the stimuli. In this experiment, the subject controlled and the experimenter recorded projection durations from the start. The procedure can probably best be described by making immediate reference to Figure 3. Note that the mean reciprocal values have been inverted on the ordinates of these graphs so that numerically high means (signifying short exposure durations) fall at low positions in the graphs. I shall deal first with the left-hand graph, which presents means of reciprocals based on data obtained during the initial or familiarization part of the study.

The stimuli were divided into six sets of three pictures each. A given

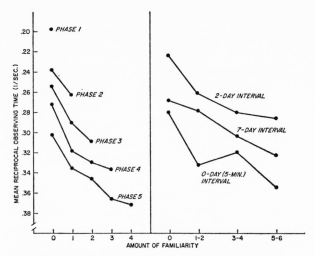

Figure 3. Mean reciprocal projection times for familiarization and test phases with counterbalancing groups combined (J. H. Cantor & G. N. Cantor, 1966). The left-hand functions are for the familiarization phases, the right-hand functions for the test phases (in the latter, one function for each of the three intervals between familiarization and testing). See text for detailed explanations of the amount-of-familiarity values ranged along the abscissas of the graphs. Reproduced from the *Journal of Experimental Psychology*, 1966, 72, 859–863, Fig. 1, by permission of the American Psychological Association.

subject first projected the three stimuli from one set; this constituted familiarization phase 1. The overall phase 1 mean is reflected in the single point plotted in the upper left-hand corner of the graph. In this stage, the particular stimuli involved were considered as having no familiarity (F_0). In phase 2, the previously seen stimuli (now regarded as having "one degree" of familiarity $-F_1$) and the three stimuli from an additional set (F_0) were projected. Thus, two means are plotted for phase 2. In similar fashion, the subject was run through three additional familiarization phases, a new set of three stimuli being added in each phase. Thus, in phase 5, five sets of stimuli ranging in familiarity value from F_0 to F_4 were projected. Turning now to the right-hand graph (test phases), five minutes following familiarization, the subject projected each of six pictures twice, one stimulus being drawn from each of the five sets already viewed and a sixth stimulus being drawn from the sixth, as yet unused set. Thus, the first time through, these stimuli had familiarity values ranging from

22

F_0 to F_5. The second time through, these same stimuli had familiarity values ranging from F_1 to F_6. This explains the meanings of the values plotted on the abscissa of the right-hand graph. The overall means for this first test phase compose the function portrayed by the bottom curve in the graph. Two days later, the *same subject* returned for a second test phase. Again, six stimuli (not involved in test phase 1) — one from each of the five sets viewed during the familiarization phases and one drawn from the sixth set — were projected twice apiece. The overall means for the second test phase are seen in the upper function in the graph. And, finally, the *same subject* returned seven days after the familiarization experience to project a final series of six pictures — that is, the remaining representative from each of the five familiarization sets plus the remaining stimulus in the sixth set. The middle function in the graph portrays the mean values obtained in the third test phase.

All subjects were treated alike in this study, except for being assigned to one of eighteen counterbalancing subgroups set up for the purpose of assuring that each of the eighteen stimuli involved contributed to each of the familiarity levels which were employed.

Turning now to the results from the familiarization phases (left-hand graph), two patterns are evident in the functions portrayed here. First, the overall projection durations decreased as the subject moved through successive familiarization phases. This is presumably attributable to an increase in general boredom across the successive familiarization phases. Secondly, within each phase involving two or more familiarity levels (phases 2–5), monotonic decreasing functions relating projection duration to familiarity level are in evidence. Nowhere does an inversion occur. With reference to the test phases (right-hand graph), note that the overall projection durations were quite short following the five-minute interval, relatively long following the two-day interval, and of moderate value following the seven-day interval. This pattern probably reflects shifting levels of general interest the task had for the subjects at the various junctures just cited. More importantly, note that, with the exception of one inversion occurring for the five-minute interval data, the patterns again reveal monotonic decreasing functions relating projection duration to familiarity level.

Separate analyses of variance applied to the familiarization data for phases 2, 3, 4, and 5 revealed a significant main effect for the amount-of-familiarity variable in each case. Follow-up tests showed that the decreases in duration from F_0 to F_1 were significant for all four of these phases. Analysis of the test phase data revealed a significant main effect for the amount-of-familiarity variable (i.e., F_0 vs. F_{1-2} vs. F_{3-4} vs. F_{5-6}), a significant main effect for interval between familiarization and testing (i.e., five minutes vs. two days vs. seven days), and a *nonsignificant* interaction between these two variables. Thus, in accord with findings from the two earlier projection studies, it may be concluded that the magnitude of the familiarity effect was not differentially altered by varying the time interval intervening between familiarization and testing. Note that, in the present study, the time interval was varied on a within-subjects basis, whereas a between-subjects manipulation occurred in the two earlier studies.

Evidence for Affective Reactions to Familiarized Stimuli

The projection data just discussed coincide with a growing body of results suggesting that, in a variety of contexts, children prefer nonfamiliarized to familiarized stimuli (see Endsley, 1967; Gullickson, 1966; Harris, 1965; Mendel, 1965; Odom, 1964).

In a recently completed study (G. N. Cantor, 1968a), I was concerned with the question of how children would rate familiarized and nonfamiliarized stimuli on a like-dislike continuum. Fifty-two fifth- and sixth-graders viewed seven four-second projections of each of ten figures taken from the Welsh Figure Preference Test and then rated these stimuli and also ten others not previously seen in the situation (see Fig. 1). For each of the twenty stimuli, the subject marked a point along a horizontal line 12.8 centimeters in length. The word *neutral* was centered beneath the line, while the anchoring terms were *strongly dislike* and *strongly like*. The words *dislike* and *like* were located on the appropriate sides of *neutral*.

The measure was simply the distance in centimeters from the strongly dislike end of the continuum to the subject's mark. Thus, the higher the score, the more favorably was the stimulus rated. The overall mean rating for the familiarized stimuli was 6.73, whereas that for the nonfamiliarized stimuli was 7.70, the difference between these means being significant at the .0001 level. Considering the average ratings given by the individual children, the mean for the nonfamiliarized stimuli was higher than that for the familiarized stimuli in the case of forty-two of the fifty-two subjects.

The final study I wish to discuss (G. N. Cantor, 1968b) was concerned with the effects of repetitive exposure to a simple visual stimulus on children's speed of responding in a simple reaction time (RT) task. The subjects were sixty first-graders, half boys and half girls. Each child alternately viewed a series of ten eight-second stimulus exposures and made a series of eight RT responses. This alternating pattern of task administrations was continued until five blocks of each had occurred. Thus, the subject experienced a total of fifty stimulus exposures and responded on a total of forty RT trials. For half the subjects, every stimulus exposure involved the same simple geometric form — a black cross on a white background; I shall refer to this as a "boredom" treatment. The remaining subjects ("non-bored") viewed fifty different colored slides, consisting mainly of action shots of children and animals. The child began each RT trial with a finger on a start button located in an anterior position on a horizontal panel. At the onset of a light stimulus, he removed his finger from the start button and depressed a response button located eight and a quarter inches from the start button in a posterior position on the same panel. Depression of the response button deactivated the light. Start and travel times on the RT task, reciprocalized to produce speed measures, were the dependent variables.

Drawing on Fowler's formulation, I expected the "boredom" treatment to raise the child's general drive level and hence to facilitate performance on what was assumed to be a simple task involving little in the way of response competition. The results are summarized in Table 6. An analysis of variance revealed the presence of a significant interaction between sex and the boredom variable. As can be seen in Table 6, the males responded faster than the females. However, although the bored males did respond faster than the non-bored males (as expected), the difference was in the opposite direction for the females. Follow-up analyses indicated that the difference was significant at the .05 level for the girls but not for the boys.

It should be pointed out that the male data were much more variable

Table 6. Mean Travel Speeds for the Four Subgroups across Eight-Trial Blocks

Sex and Group	Trial Block					
	1	2	3	4	5	Overall
Male						
Non-bored	3.400	3.304	3.113	3.193	3.189	3.240
Bored	3.554	3.654	3.669	3.807	3.521	3.641
Female						
Non-bored	2.927	3.101	3.077	3.112	3.001	3.044
Bored	2.795	2.733	2.564	2.506	2.503	2.620

SOURCE: G. N. Cantor, 1968b.

than were the female. This fact, coupled with the consistency with which the boredom difference occurred across trial blocks for the males, suggests that an enhancement effect from boredom in this kind of situation may be a replicable finding, at least for boys. The results for the females are quite contrary to what one might expect on the basis of tedium theories such as Fowler's. It is possible that boredom led to response competition in the female subjects, but such an interpretation is difficult to reconcile with the fact that an effect for females was found for travel and not starting speeds. Were response competition involved, it seems reasonable to argue that the start speed measure would have been as sensitive as travel speed to such an effect, if not more so.

Overview of the Stimulus Familiarization Data

Perhaps the most striking thing about the various data I have considered here is the fact that, in rather different contexts, reliable effects have been demonstrated due to very limited familiarization treatments. When compared with the numbers and durations of stimulus exposures experienced by children in everyday life, the amounts of familiarization given to the subjects in these laboratory studies must be considered modest, indeed. And yet, effects stemming from such treatments were demonstrable. With reference to the projection studies, it is most surprising that familiarization effects of comparable magnitudes were obtained when testing occurred five minutes, two days, and seven days following familiarization. One must acknowledge, it seems to me, that this is a variable with effects of some considerable durability. I have already commented in detail on theoretical considerations relating to the SFE. If the SFE data have any psychological significance at all, it seems likely that their value will take the form of implications for habituation and OR theorizing.

In the ensuing remarks, I should like to comment generally on the projection, rating, and boredom studies. We are concerned here, first of all, with a pervasive and perplexing question, Do children prefer familiar or nonfamiliar stimulation? Folklore stresses the desirability of familiarity, especially in the case of young children. Yet, as I believe has been amply documented in the present paper, it is not difficult to demonstrate a preference on the part of fairly young children for nonfamiliar stimulation in the laboratory setting.

It seems likely that the question, as posed above, has no single or simple answer. Potentially relevant variables that immediately come to mind include the age of the child, the amount of familiarization the child has experienced, the complexity level of the stimuli in question, and, probably most important, the kinds of experiential events (e.g., pleasant or unpleasant) the child associates with familiarized stimuli. Taking these (and probably other) variables into account, it appears reasonable to guess that preferences in either direction are demonstrable. The need for systematic manipulation of such variables in an extensive program of research directed at the preference issue is apparent.

The projection and rating data reported here do suggest that, under the experimental conditions involved, children will show a preference for nonfamiliarized stimuli. Such findings, though by no means conclusive, do add credence to viewpoints such as Fowler's to the effect that a familiar stimulus is a tedium-producing stimulus and/or that an unfamiliar stimulus can have incentive value.

The question of the functional properties of the state ordinarily called "boredom" strikes me as constituting the most interesting and theoretically significant problem dealt with in any of the studies considered above. The one directly relevant study (Cantor, 1968b) barely scratches the surface, and its results can be considered only suggestive, at best. The assumption that the "bored" child is a "driven" child conforms very well to common sense impressions. Yet, when my colleagues and I deliberately set out to "bore" the child, we produced effects by no means entirely consistent with our expectations. If Fowler's theory is correct, we should be able to demonstrate that boring a child enhances his performance in a simple, non-competitional task situation. An extended string of failures in this regard would surely render questionable the utility of "tedium" theories and might even have implications for the viability of the generalized drive construct — a concept increasingly coming under attack by contemporary behavior theorists (e.g., Bolles, 1958; Estes, 1958; Maltzman & Raskin, 1965).

I shall conclude with the following assertions. The field of developmental psychology has as its major raison d'être the fact that children of different ages respond differently to the same stimuli occurring in their environment. Among our principal jobs as developmentalists is the task of reaching an understanding of the mechanisms underlying such differences. One of the important mechanisms involved has to do, I submit, with the familiarization variable. At the risk of sounding unprofound, I would argue that older children respond differently to the world than do younger children (some might wish to say they "perceive the world differently") at least partly because they have simply been looking at it longer.

References

Berlyne, D. E. *Conflict, arousal, and curiosity.* New York: McGraw-Hill, 1960.

Bogartz, R. S., & K. L. Witte. On the locus of the stimulus familiarization effect in young children. *Journal of Experimental Child Psychology*, 1966, 4, 317–331.

Bolles, R. C. The usefulness of the drive concept, in M. R. Jones, ed., *Nebraska symposium on motivation.* Lincoln: University of Nebraska Press, 1958.

Brown, J. S. *The motivation of behavior.* New York: McGraw-Hill, 1961.

Butler, R. A. Discrimination learning by rhesus monkeys to visual-exploration motivation. *Journal of Comparative and Physiological Psychology*, 1953, 46, 95–98.

Cantor, G. N. Children's "like-dislike" ratings of familiarized and nonfamiliarized visual stimuli. *Journal of Experimental Child Psychology*, 1968, 6, 651–657. (a)

————. Effects of a "boredom" treatment on children's simple RT performance. *Psychonomic Science*, 1968, 10, 299–300. (b)

———— & J. H. Cantor. Effects of conditioned-stimulus familiarization on instrumental learning in children. *Journal of Experimental Child Psychology*, 1964, 1, 71–78.

————. Discriminative reaction time performance in preschool children as related to stimulus familiarization. *Journal of Experimental Child Psychology*, 1965, 2, 1–9.

————. Discriminative reaction time in children as related to amount of stimulus familiarization. *Journal of Experimental Child Psychology*, 1966, 4, 150–157.

Cantor, G. N., & L. Fenson. New data regarding the relationship of amount of familiarization to the stimulus familiarization effect (SFE). *Journal of Experimental Child Psychology*, 1968, 6, 167–173.

Cantor, J. H., & G. N. Cantor. Children's observing behavior as related to amount and recency of stimulus familiarization. *Journal of Experimental Child Psychology*, 1964, 1, 241–247. (a)

————. Observing behavior in children as a function of stimulus novelty. *Child Development*, 1964, 35, 119–128. (b)

————. Functions relating children's observing behavior to amount and recency of stimulus familiarization. *Journal of Experimental Psychology*, 1966, 72, 859–863.

Dember, W. N. Alternation behavior, in D. W. Fiske & S. R. Maddi, eds., *Functions of varied experience.* Homewood, Ill.: Dorsey Press, 1961.

Endsley, R. C. Effects of differential prior exposure on preschool children's subsequent choice of novel stimuli. *Psychonomic Science*, 1967, 7, 411–412.

Estes, W. K. Stimulus-response theory of drive, in M. R. Jones, ed., *Nebraska symposium on motivation.* Lincoln: University of Nebraska Press, 1958.

Fowler, H. Satiation and curiosity: Constructs for a drive and incentive-motivation theory of exploration, in K. W. Spence & J. T. Spence, eds., *The psychology of learning and motivation: Advances in research and theory*, Vol. 1. New York: Academic Press, 1967.

Glanzer, M. Stimulus satiation: An explanation of spontaneous alternation and related phenomena. *Psychological Review*, 1953, 60, 257–268.

Gullickson, G. R. A note on children's selection of novel auditory stimuli. *Journal of Experimental Child Psychology*, 1966, 4, 158–162.

Harlow, H. F. Motivation as a factor in the acquisition of new responses, in J. S. Brown, H. F. Harlow, L. J. Postman, V. Nowlis, T. M. Newcomb, & O. H. Mowrer, *Current theory and research in motivation: A symposium.* Lincoln: University of Nebraska Press, 1953.

Harris, L. The effects of relative novelty on children's choice behavior. *Journal of Experimental Child Psychology,* 1965, 2, 297–305.

Leuba, C. Toward some integration of learning theories: The concept of optimal stimulation. *Psychological Reports,* 1955, 1, 27–33.

Lynn, R. *Attention, arousal and the orientation reaction.* New York: Pergamon Press, 1966.

Maltzman, I. Individual differences in "attention": The orienting reflex, in R. M. Gagné, ed., *Learning and individual differences.* Columbus, Ohio: Merrill, 1967.
———, & D. C. Raskin. Effects of individual differences in the orienting reflex on conditioning and complex processes. *Journal of Experimental Research in Personality,* 1965, 1, 1–16.
———, O. Johnson, & J. Gould. Reaction time and the conditioned orienting reflex under different conditioned-stimulus–unconditioned-stimulus intervals. *Proceedings of the 73rd Annual Convention of the American Psychological Association,* 1965, pp. 5–6.

Mendel, G. Children's preferences for differing degrees of novelty. *Child Development,* 1965, 36, 453–465.

Meyers, W. J., & L. J. Joseph. Response speed as related to CS-prefamiliarization and GSR-responsivity. *Journal of Experimental Psychology,* 1968, 78, 375–381.

Miller, F. D. The effects of differential amounts of stimulus familiarization on discriminative reaction time performance in children. Ph.D. thesis, University of Iowa, 1966.

Montgomery, K. C. The role of the exploratory drive in learning. *Journal of Comparative and Physiological Psychology,* 1954, 47, 60–64.

Myers, A. K., & N. E. Miller. Failure to find a learned drive based on hunger: Evidence for learning motivated by "exploration." *Journal of Comparative and Physiological Psychology,* 1954, 47, 428–436.

O'Connell, R. H. Trials with tedium and titillation. *Psychological Bulletin,* 1965, 63, 170–179.

Odom, R. D. Effects of auditory and visual stimulus deprivation and satiation on children's performance in an operant task. *Journal of Experimental Child Psychology,* 1964, 1, 16–25.

Sokolov, E. N. *Perception and the conditioned reflex.* New York: Pergamon Press, 1963.
———. The measurement of sensitivity and reactivity of a conditioned reflex arc in connection with the interaction of orienting and defense reactions, in L. G. Voronin, A. N. Leontiev, A. R. Luria, E. N. Sokolov, & O. S. Vinogradova, eds., *Orienting reflex and exploratory behavior.* Washington, D.C.: American Institute of Biological Sciences, 1965.

Spiker, C. C. The concept of development: Relevant and irrelevant issues, in H. W. Stevenson, ed., A report of a conference commemorating the fortieth anniversary of the Institute of Child Development, University of Minnesota. *Monographs of the Society for Research in Child Development,* 1966, 31 (5, Serial No. 107), 40–54.

Thompson, R. F., & W. A. Spencer. Habituation: A model phenomenon for the study of neuronal substrates of behavior. *Psychological Review,* 1966, 73, 16–43.

Welsh, G. S. *Welsh Figure Preference Test* (research ed.). Palo Alto, Calif.: Consulting Psychologists Press, 1959.

Wickens, D. D. The orienting reflex and attention, in R. M. Gagné, ed., *Learning and individual differences.* Columbus, Ohio.: Merrill, 1967.

Witte, K. L. Children's instrumental response speeds as related to conditioned-stimulus duration during a familiarization experience. M.A. thesis, University of Iowa, 1965.

———. Children's response speeds to familiarized stimuli. *Psychonomic Science,* 1967, 7, 153–154.

———, & G. N. Cantor. Children's response speeds to the offset of novel and familiar stimuli. *Journal of Experimental Child Psychology,* 1967, 5, 372–380.

◆ VICTOR H. DENENBERG ◆

Animal Studies of Early Experience
Some Principles Which Have Implications
for Human Development

IN THIS paper I shall discuss some animal studies within the context of early experience research. I do not intend to review the extensive literature that has grown up within the past ten to fifteen years, since that is better read than talked about (for recent reviews see Denenberg, 1962; 1964; 1966; Newton & Levine, 1968). Instead, I have deliberately selected a few animal experiments to demonstrate several important principles — principles which, I believe, have considerable generality throughout the mammalian kingdom, including the human.

Early Experience Research in Breadth:
From Mouse to Man

The early experience research described below has been done with the mouse, the rat, the dog, the monkey, and man. Not only do these studies differ with respect to the species involved, they also differ in the independent variables manipulated and the end points measured. The sections below should not be looked upon as an attempt to place this research into a comparative psychology context. However, in spite of, or possibly because of, the vast differences among these studies, I believe that there emerge the important principles which are discussed in the second half of this paper.

NOTE: Much of the research described in this paper was supported, in part, by Research Grant HD-02068 from the National Institute of Child Health and Human Development, National Institutes of Health.

31

MOUSE

A common characteristic of a number of strains of mice is that the males, when mature, will fight spontaneously. Because this behavior occurs naturally in the species, it seems reasonable to conclude that there is a genetic basis for this behavior and that aggression is ethologically meaningful — that is, serves some biological function — for the animal.

Briefly, aggressive behavior is measured by removing adult males from colony cages and isolating them in mouse boxes for approximately one week. Unlimited food and water are available. At the end of this time two males are introduced to each other; their behavior is observed five minutes daily for about a week. The mice will initially explore the "fighting box," groom themselves, possibly groom each other, and then they may attack each other. In the colony of C57BL/10 mice at Purdue, roughly 35 to 60 per cent of the pairs of any particular sample will engage in one or more fights under these conditions. The fights can become vicious, and one of the animals may be severely injured or killed unless the fighters are separated. Animals are routinely separated after ten seconds of fighting.

One of the major variables which my colleagues and I have been studying with respect to its effects upon aggressive behavior is the nature of the mother which rears the mouse pup. We have manipulated the maternal variable by fostering four-day-old mouse pups to lactating rat mothers that have been nursing their rat pups for approximately four days (Denenberg, Hudgens, & Zarrow, 1964; 1966; Hudgens, Denenberg, & Zarrow, 1967). In some instances we have fostered complete litters of mice so that each mouse has its own siblings as peers and the only variable is the nature of the mother. In other instances, we have fostered one or two mice to a lactating rat mother who keeps several of her pups — thus the mouse is exposed to both rat mothers and rat peers.

The relevant finding for this discussion is that when mice are reared by rat mothers until weaning, and then tested in adulthood in the fighting situation, the probability of a fight occurring is almost zero (Denenberg et al., 1964; 1966; Hudgens et al., 1967). Putting it simply, by changing the nature of the mother rearing the mouse, the incidence of fighting is reduced from 35–60 per cent to 0–10 per cent in the studies we have completed so far.

RAT

In an experiment with rats, Cooper and Zubek (1958) asked the important question, What are the consequences of enriched and restricted environments in early life upon the problem-solving performance of maze-bright and maze-dull rats? The subjects were animals from the McGill bright and dull strains. At the time of weaning the animals were placed into one of three environments: a Hebb-type enriched free environment containing ramps, mirrors, swings, polished balls, marbles, barriers, slides, tunnels, bells, teeter-totters, and springboards, in addition to food boxes and water pans; a restricted environment consisting of a bare cage except for food box and water pan; or a normal laboratory environment. The animals were maintained in these quarters from weaning at twenty-five days until they were sixty-five days old, when testing on the Hebb-Williams maze began. Cooper and Zubek's results — the number of errors made by the rats in the maze — can be summarized thus:

Genetics	Normal Environment	Enriched Environment	Restricted Environment
Maze-bright rats	117.0	111.2	169.7
Maze-dull rats	164.0	119.7	169.5

Looking first at animals reared in the normal environment, we see that the usual differences between maze-bright and maze-dull animals are obtained, with the bright animals making 117 errors on the average over the twelve problems and the dull animals making 164 errors. When both groups are reared in an enriched environment, the reduction in the number of errors for the bright animals is negligible, but the reduction in errors for the dull group is considerable — to the point where the difference between the groups is no longer significant. However, the consequences of rearing in a restricted environment are that both groups have approximately 170 errors. The restricted condition had a deleterious effect upon the maze-bright rats but an insignificant effect upon the maze-dull animals.

The first thing to note about these impressive findings is that as great a difference in behavioral variance was obtained by manipulating the early experiences of these rats as was possible by genetic selection through thirteen generations. The mean difference between the bright and dull groups in the normal environment was 44 points, which reflects the difference brought about by genetic selection. On the other hand, within the bright group the range of scores for different environments is 58 points whereas the range is 50 points within the dull group. In both cases this behavioral variance is brought about by the nature of the environment.

DOG

The experiment with the dog also stemmed from Hebb's (1949) theoretical influence. This is the fascinating study by Melzack and Scott (1957), in which Scottish terriers were raised in restricted isolation from puppyhood until maturity. They were reared in cages which deprived them of normal sensory and social experience between weaning at four weeks of age until removal at eight months of age. The comparison groups of animals were either reared in the laboratory under normal conditions or in private homes.

Melzack and Scott were interested in the ability of their animals to respond to painful stimuli. In two experiments in which the animals had to learn to avoid electrical shock, the restricted animals required four times as many trials as the controls before they made the appropriate avoidance response.

The most dramatic findings concerned the response of the two groups of dogs to being burnt by a match or pricked by a pin. The procedure was for the experimenter to attempt to push a burning match into the dog's nose or to jab a dissecting needle into the skin of the animals. Predictably, once the free-environment animals had been subjected to pain, they kept away from the experimenter. Amazingly, of the ten restricted dogs which had their noses burnt, nine spent more time near the experimenter after nose burning than before, and six of the eight restricted dogs which were pricked with a pin spent more time near the experimenter after this occurred. The description of the behavior of the restricted dogs to nose burning is worth quoting (Melzack & Scott, 1957, p. 158):

To the astonishment of the observers, seven of the ten restricted dogs made no attempt to get away from *E* during stimulation and it was not even necessary to hold them. The sequence of behavior observed was almost identical for all seven dogs: they moved their noses into the flame as soon as it was presented, after which the head or whole body jerked away, as though reflexively; but then they came right back to their original position and hovered excitedly near the flame. Three of them repeatedly poked their noses into the flame and sniffed at it as long as it was present. If they snuffed it out, another match was struck, and the same sequence of events occurred. The other four did not sniff at the match, but offered no resistance nor made any attempt to get away after the first contact, and *E* was able to touch these dogs' noses with the flame as often as he wished.

In brief, early restriction of social and sensory experiences is sufficient to eliminate the normal escape response to noxious stimuli. (For an excellent review of the literature on early deprivation in mammals, see Bronfenbrenner, 1968.)

MONKEY

The experiments with monkeys reported here took place at Harlow's laboratory in Wisconsin. Beginning with Mason's report in 1960, there has been clear documentation that monkeys raised in social isolation from birth until adulthood are incapable or less capable of performing the basic steps required in sexual intercourse (Harlow, 1962; Harlow & Harlow, 1962). Fortunately, the lack of social interaction did not eliminate all coping behavior and with the guidance and encouragement of the experimenters some of the females did copulate and become pregnant. This gave Harlow and his students the opportunity to study the maternal behavior of these motherless monkeys (Arling & Harlow, 1967; Seay, Alexander, & Harlow, 1964). In the Seay et al. (1964) paper four experimental mothers all reacted with indifference or abusiveness toward their infants. In the replication by Arling and Harlow, only two of the four females acted in this fashion, and eventually one of these became reasonably maternal in her behavior. Despite the difference in qualitative behavior between the two experiments, the same general quantitative findings were obtained in that the motherless mothers were distinctly deficient in basic patterns of maternal behavior when compared with feral-reared mothers.

In brief, then, social isolation from birth onward in the rhesus monkey results in a marked reduction in sexual competence, and, when the female does become pregnant and has a baby, there is also a marked deficiency in maternal behavior.

MAN

Let me describe two anthropological studies. The first, by Landauer and Whiting (1964), is concerned with the relation between stress in infancy and height of adult males. The stimulus for this study was findings from early experience research with animals that stressful stimulation in infancy led to a more rapid rate of physical growth (Denenberg & Karas, 1959; 1961; Levine, 1962). Landauer and Whiting used height as their measure of physical growth and did a cross-cultural analysis relating this to stressful infant-care practices. Two classes of stressors were used: piercing and molding. In their first sample Landauer and Whiting found that those societies in which infants received stress during their first two years of life produced males which were 2.49 inches taller in adulthood than did societies where such experiences of stress were absent. In an independent cross-validation, males from societies which practiced piercing or molding during the first two years of life were 2.64 inches taller than males from societies without such practices. A similar pattern of results was obtained when comparing the adult height of American children inoculated before and after two years of age (Whiting, Landauer, & Jones, 1968).

In another report, Whiting (1965) studied the relation between stress during the first two weeks of life and onset of menarche. The median age of menarche was 12.25 years in societies in which the females were subjected to either pain or shaping, whereas the median age was 14.0 years in those societies where such stressful events did not occur. There appears to be an interesting parallel between Whiting's findings and those of Morton, Denenberg, and Zarrow (1963), who found that sexual maturation occurred earlier in both male and female rats if they had been handled in infancy.

A summary of the salient aspects of the studies discussed above appears below.

Summary of Findings of Early Experience Research with Five Species of Mammals

Species	Independent Variable	Effects upon End Points
Mouse	Nature of mother and peer.	Rearing by rat mothers reduced aggression.
Rat	Genetic: maze bright or maze dull. Restricted, normal, or enriched environment.	Enriched environment improved problem-solving of maze dulls. Restricted environment depressed performance of maze brights.
Dog	Restricted environment.	Inability to perceive and escape from painful stimuli.
Monkey	Maternal and peer deprivation.	Incompetence or inability to engage in sexual behavior. Deficient maternal behavior.
Man	Stress.	Male adult height greater if stressed in infancy. Menarche earlier for stressed females.

Principles

I. GENETICALLY BASED CHARACTERS MAY BE DRASTICALLY MODIFIED BY EARLY EXPERIENCES

The common element among these studies is certainly not the species involved nor the experimental treatments administered. Nor are any immediate relations seen when one considers the criterion measures used:

aggression, problem-solving, pain perception, sexual behavior, maternal behavior, height of adult males, and onset of menarche. Yet if one moves up to a higher level of abstraction, it may be shown that these diverse end points do have several very important elements in common: namely, all these end points have a strong genetic base. In addition, the behavioral end points all have adaptive value in the evolutionary sense of aiding in the survival of the organism or the species.

In the mouse, *aggressive behavior* occurs spontaneously and thus may be considered to be species-specific. It is unquestionably of adaptive value in helping the animal survive in a wild state.

The genetic basis of maze learning and *problem-solving* in the rat has been shown by selection experiments ever since Tryon's (1940). It is quite reasonable to assume that an animal with greater capability for learning and solving problems would have a better chance of adapting to his environment and thus surviving. In fact, one of the unique characteristics of the human is his tremendous learning and problem-solving capabilities.

If an animal is to survive in its ecological niche, where it is certain to be subjected to the attacks of predators, possible lack of food and water, and extremes in environmental temperature, it is apparent that the animal must have a keen *sense of pain*. Indeed, it is difficult to think of a mammalian organism that could survive, even in a highly civilized human world, without any pain sensitivity at all.

The adaptive value of *sexual and maternal behavior* is readily apparent. Without sexual behavior a species cannot reproduce itself. Even with sexual behavior, if there is no maternal behavior, the species cannot survive.

It is not so easy to show that *adult height* and earlier *onset of menarche* may have adaptive value for the human. However, the genetic basis of height has been well established in a variety of research reports, and the genetic basis of menarche is evident since this is related to the sex chromosome.

From these data comes my first principle: Behaviors which have fundamental adaptive evolutionary meaning to the animal and behaviors or morphological characters which have a strong genetic basis are amenable to drastic modification by the appropriate manipulations of an animal's experiences during early development.

II. EARLY EXPERIENCES HAVE LONG-TERM CONSEQUENCES

The second principle which I wish to establish, and one which is implicit in the data discussed above, is that the effects of early experiences have long-term consequences. This is not a simple transitory phenomenon but, instead, a very robust effect which can modify an animal's behavior for its complete lifetime, and may even affect the offspring and the grandchildren of such animals (Denenberg & Rosenberg, 1967; Denenberg & Whimbey, 1963).

The Long-Term Consequences of Early Stimulation for a Variety of Species

Species	Variable	Age of Early Stimulation	Test Age
Mouse	Aggression	1–21 days	105 days
Rat	Problem-solving	1–21, 22–50, or 1–50 days	371 days
Rat	Timidity	5–24 days	544–565 days
Dog	Avoidance learning	Puppyhood to maturity	2 yrs. later
Monkey	Sexual behavior	First 7–12 mo.	3 yrs., 1 mo. to 4 yrs., 4 mo.
Man	Height	First 2 yrs.	16 yrs. (est.)
Man	Onset of menarche	1–14 days	12 yrs., 3 mo.

Effects upon the Animal. The summary above illustrates the relation between age of stimulation and test age for a variety of species. In the mouse data described above, the experimental animals were reared with rat mothers until weaning at 3 weeks of age. The test for aggressive behavior took place after the animals were sexually mature (average age for oldest group tested was 105 days).

In the Cooper and Zubeck study of maze-bright and maze-dull rats, the animals were tested as soon as they were removed from their respective environments, and so there is no evidence of long-term effects here. However, recently Denenberg, Woodcock, and Rosenberg (1968) studied a group of experimental rats born and reared in a free environment until weaning, a second group born in standard maternity cages and kept in a free environment from weaning until fifty days of age, and a third group born and reared in the free environment for all the first fifty days of life. The control group, of course, were born in standard maternity cages and then placed into laboratory cages at the time of weaning. After fifty days of age all experimental animals were put in standard laboratory cages where they remained until a year old, when they were taken out to be tested in the Hebb-Williams maze. Even ten months after the termination of their free-environment experience, all three experimental groups were found to perform significantly better on problem-solving than the control group.

An experiment which really pushed the limits of the age question was one by Hunt and Otis (1963), who subjected rats to different forms of stimulation in infancy. One group of these animals was not tested until at least 544 days old at which time Hunt and Otis found that the stimulated animals were less timid than were rats that had not been disturbed in infancy.

The restricted dogs in the Melzack and Scott study were released from restriction after their testing and were reared normally in the laboratory for the next two years. At that time they were retested and were found still to be markedly deficient in learning to avoid shock.

Harlow, Harlow, Dodsworth, and Arling (1966) report that female monkeys raised in semi-isolation during infancy were still unable to engage in appropriate sexual behavior at 4 years and 4 months of age.

Finally, Landauer and Whiting's (1964) end point was the average height of adult males so it is reasonable to assume a gap of at least 14 years between the termination of the early stress experience and the measurement of height. And in the Whiting (1965) paper concerning the onset of menarche, the earliest average age reported was 12 years and 3 months.

Effects upon the Animal's Progeny. Thus, stimulation in early life has extremely long-term consequences for the animal's behavior. Moreover, this effect is powerful enough to have impact upon yet-to-be-born progeny, at least in the rat and mouse. Denenberg and Whimbey (1963) demonstrated that weaning weight and open-field performance of rats were significantly modified by the experiences which their mothers had had when the mothers were infants. Denenberg and Rosenberg (1967) extended this phenomenon and have shown that differential experiences in the early life of female rats will significantly modify their grandpups' behavior in an open field. And Ginsburg and Hovda (1947), by transplanting fertilized ova from one mouse strain to another, showed that the nature of the uterine and maternal environment could influence the percentage of deaths caused by audiogenic seizures in the descendents.

The Question of Irreversibility. Let me emphasize that the evidence presented above says nothing about whether the effects of early experience are reversible or not. In most of the studies which I have described the animals have been maintained under rather constant and standardized laboratory conditions until the time of testing, and "therapy" has not been introduced in an attempt to modify the animal's behavior. (An exception to this is seen in the studies of Harlow in which various therapeutic procedures were often found to be ineffective.) It is quite dangerous to overgeneralize from these results to conclude that these effects are irreversible until the proper studies have clearly established this point (and the problem of proving the null hypothesis would still remain).

III. EARLY EXPERIENCES ARE ONE MAJOR CAUSE
OF INDIVIDUAL DIFFERENCES

A third principle, which is also inherent in the material discussed above, is that differential early experiences are a significant cause of individual differences among animals. Aggression, problem-solving ability, pain perception, sexual behavior, maternal behavior, height, and onset of menarche are all affected by early experiences, and the measurement of these kinds of behaviors is the stock in trade of the differential psychologist. Although this third principle is almost a truism, its importance lies in suggesting that one can use experimental methods to investigate causes of individual differences. My colleagues and I have been engaged in such a research program for several years.

The research has involved "programing life histories" in the rat. We asked the question, What are important experiences which occur in a developing organism, and how do these experiences act, singly and in combination, to affect the organism's performance in adulthood? We decided to manipulate two major classes of experiences, social and stress. This was done by writing out, or programing, different schedules of experiences for different groups of rats, starting with the nature of their mother (emotional or nonemotional) and going through the first two hundred days of their lives. We have usually worked with a 2^n factorial design in which the independent variables are the occurrence or nonoccurrence (usually) of a particular experience at some point in an animal's developmental history. Such an experiment is usually evaluated by means of an analysis of variance. However, if one considers only the mean of a particular experimental group, one has an idealized individual in the sense that this group mean is freed from genetic variance (because animals are randomly assigned to treatment conditions) and the experiential causes of the animal's behavior (i.e., group mean) are known by examining his particular program of life experiences (Denenberg, 1967; Whimbey & Denenberg, 1967).

If one takes a large number of these idealized individuals and administers a battery of tests to them, he can obtain the intercorrelations among these tests and factor analyze them in an R-type factor analysis. Whimbey & Denenberg (1966; 1967) have been able to isolate a meaningful factor structure from such an analysis. They (1967) have also done a Q-type analysis to determine the nature of the clusterings of the independent variables (in this case, our experimental treatments). A discussion of these results would be too long to include here. Suffice it to say that meaningful factors emerged from the analyses, thus establishing that significant "individual differences" can be created by experimental means independent of any contribution from genetic variance.

IV. EARLY EXPERIENCES HAVE MULTIPLE EFFECTS

My fourth principle is that stimulation in early life affects a multiplicity of biological and behavioral processes, rather than affecting only one or two processes. For example, mice reared by lactating rat mothers differ with respect to aggressive behavior, open-field activity, body weight, social preference, and adrenocortical activity (Denenberg et al., 1964; 1966; Denenberg, Rosenberg, Paschke, Hess, Zarrow, & Levine, 1968; Hudgens et al., 1967). As another example, handling of rats in infancy modifies their body weight, adrenosteroid response, emotionality, exploratory behavior, ingestive behavior, avoidance learning, social preference, and capability of withstanding stresses (Denenberg, 1967; Levine, Haltmeyer, Karas, & Denenberg, 1967).

V. THE AGE WHEN STIMULATION IS ADMINISTERED IS CRUCIAL

My final principle is that the age at which stimulation is administered in infancy is extremely crucial. For example, handling the rat after weaning does not have the same consequences as handling the rat during the first three weeks of life (Levine, 1956; Levine & Otis, 1958). Also, the procedure of gentling rats immediately after weaning, which appears to be somewhat akin to the handling procedure, has not been shown to have meaningful long-term consequences, though the initial research on this subject was promising (Ader, 1959; Bernstein, 1952; 1957; Levine & Otis, 1958; Mogenson & Ehrlich, 1958; Scott, 1955; Weininger, 1956).

This does not mean that the *earliest* experiences are the most important.

41

For example, Denenberg, Woodcock, and Rosenberg (1968) found that Hebb-Williams problem-solving behavior was improved more by free environment experience during the second three weeks of life than during the first three weeks of life. Forgays and Read (1962) reported the same finding.

I should like to repeat here a generality about age and stimulation, based upon research with the rat (Denenberg, 1966). Stimulation before weaning appears to have its greatest effect upon affective-emotional behaviors, whereas stimulation after weaning is more likely to modify cognitive functions. Pre-weaning stimulation (including handling) has impact upon an animal's emotional reactivity, its ability to learn using noxious reinforcers, its adrenal physiology, and so forth. However, handling has no effect upon Hebb-Williams problem-solving behavior (Denenberg & Morton, 1962; Schaefer, 1963). On the other hand, free-environment experience after weaning has been shown to have a powerful and permanent effect upon problem-solving behavior.

This is not to say that pre-weaning stimulation affects only emotional processes and that post-weaning stimulation affects only cognitive processes. Rather, pre-weaning stimulation has a relatively greater impact upon affective than cognitive processes, whereas post-weaning stimulation plays the opposite role. It should be emphasized that this statement is more in the nature of a hypothesis to be tested than a firmly established principle.

Finally, within the context of a discussion of the variable of age, one must make note of the concept of critical periods. This is too complicated a topic to discuss now except to reiterate my position "that it is more reasonable to study the functional relationships among various classes of independent and dependent variables between birth and weaning than to design experiments which try to isolate critical periods during the developmental period between birth and weaning" (Denenberg, 1968, p. 165). For a more extended discussion of the critical period concept see Denenberg (1964; 1968), Scott (1958; 1962), and Scott and Marston (1950).

Implications

I wish to stress that we are just beginning to realize the implications of the animal studies in early experience. We are just beginning to become aware of the long-term dramatic changes which can be brought about in an animal's behavior pattern and its physiological and morphological nature by appropriate interventions in early life. When one is able to modify behaviors as fundamental as sex, pain perception, fighting, problem-solving, and so forth in such a drastic fashion, he begins to appreciate that manipulations of early experience may be one of the most powerful methods of modifying behavioral variance in mammals, including the human.

I have a strong personal conviction, based upon a large amount of animal data, that the human infant's experiences during his first two years of life may have equally profound effects upon his future behavioral and physiological competence. I suspect that the analogue of pre-weaning stimulation (e.g., handling) in the rat is represented in the human during the first four to twenty-four weeks of life. I also suspect that the analogue to successful use of the Hebb-type enriched environment in the rat begins at roughly six months of age in the human. Finally, if real progress is to be made in understanding ontogeny of human development, I believe that it is absolutely necessary for those working with animals and those working with the human to collaborate in active research programs for their own mutual benefit as well as for the benefit of future generations.

References

Ader, R. The effects of early experience on subsequent emotionality and resistance to stress. *Psychological Monographs*, 1959, 73 (2, Whole No. 472), 1–31.
Arling, G. L., & H. F. Harlow. Effects of social deprivation on maternal behavior of rhesus monkeys. *Journal of Comparative Physiological Psychology*, 1967, 64, 371–377.
Bernstein, L. A note on Christie's "Experimental naivete and experiential naivete." *Psychological Bulletin*, 1952, 49, 38–40.
———. The effects of variations in handling upon learning and retention. *Journal of Comparative Physiological Psychology*, 1957, 50, 162–167.
Bronfenbrenner, U. Early deprivation in mammals: A cross-species analysis, in G. Newton & S. Levine, eds., *Early experience and behavior*, pp. 627–764. Springfield, Ill.: Thomas, 1968.
Cooper, R. M., & J. P. Zubek. Effects of enriched and restricted early environments on the learning ability of bright and dull rats. *Canadian Journal of Psychology*, 1958, 12, 159–164.
Denenberg, V. H. The effects of early experience, in E. S. E. Hafez, ed., *The behavior of domestic animals*, pp. 109–138. London: Bailliere, Tindall, & Cox, 1962.
———. Critical periods, stimulus input, and emotional reactivity: A theory of infantile stimulation. *Psychological Review*, 1964, 71, 335–351.
———. Animal studies on developmental determinants of behavioral adaptability, in O. J. Harvey, ed., Experience, structure, and adaptability, pp. 123–148. New York: Springer, 1966.
———. Stimulation in infancy, emotional reactivity, and exploratory behavior, in D. C. Glass, ed., *Neurophysiology and emotion*, pp. 161–190. New York: Rockefeller University Press and Russell Sage Foundation, 1967.
———. A consideration of the usefulness of the critical period hypothesis as applied

to the stimulation of rodents in infancy, in G. Newton & S. Levine, eds., *Early experience and behavior*, pp. 142–167. Springfield, Ill.: Thomas, 1968.

———, G. A. Hudgens, & M. X. Zarrow. Mice reared with rats: Modification of behavior by early experience with another species. *Science*, 1964, 143, 380–381.

———. Mice reared with rats: Effects of mother on adult behavior patterns. *Psychological Report*, 1966, 18, 451–456.

Denenberg, V. H., & Karas, G. G. Effects of differential infantile handling upon weight gain and mortality in the rat and mouse. *Science*, 1959, 130, 629–630.

———. The interactive effects of infantile and adult experiences upon weight gain and mortality in the rat. *Journal of Comparative Physiological Psychology*, 1961, 54, 685–689.

Denenberg, V. H., & J. R. C. Morton. Effects of preweaning and postweaning manipulations upon problem-solving behavior. *Journal of Comparative Physiological Psychology*, 1962, 55, 1096–1098.

Denenberg, V. H., & K. M. Rosenberg. Nongenetic transmission of information. *Nature*, 1967, 216, 549–550.

———, R. Paschke, J. L. Hess, M. X. Zarrow, & S. Levine. Plasma corticosterone levels as a function of cross-species fostering and species differences. *Endocrinology*, 1968, 83, 900–902.

Denenberg, V. H., & A. E. Whimbey. Behavior of adult rats is modified by the experiences their mothers had as infants. *Science*, 1963, 142, 1192–1193.

Denenberg, V. H., J. M. Woodcock, & K. M. Rosenberg. Long-term effects of preweaning and postweaning free-environment experience on the rat's problem solving behavior. *Journal of Comparative Physiological Psychology*, 1968, 66, 533–535.

Forgays, D. G., & J. M. Read. Crucial periods for free-environmental experience in the rat. *Journal of Comparative Physiological Psychology*, 1962, 55, 816–818.

Ginsburg, B. E., & R. B. Hovda. On the physiology of gene controlled audiogenic seizures in mice. *Anatomical Record*, 1947, 99, 621–622.

Harlow, H. F. The heterosexual affectional system in monkeys. *American Psychologist*, 1962, 17, 1–9.

———, & M. K. Harlow. Social deprivation in monkeys. *Scientific American*, 1962, 207, 136–146.

———, R. O. Dodsworth, & G. L. Arling. Maternal behavior of rhesus monkeys deprived of mothering and peer associations in infancy. *Proceedings of the American Philosophical Society*, 1966, 110, 58–66.

Hebb, D. O. *The organization of behavior*. New York: Wiley, 1949.

Hudgens, G. A., V. H. Denenberg, & M. X. Zarrow. Mice reared with rats: Relations between mothers' activity level and offspring's behavior. *Journal of Comparative Physiological Psychology*, 1967, 63, 304–308.

Hunt, H. F., & L. S. Otis. Early "experience" and its effects on later behavioral processes in rats: I. Initial experiments. *Transactions of the New York Academy of Sciences*, 1963, 25, 858–870.

Landauer, T. K., & J. W. Whiting. Infantile stimulation and adult stature of human males. *American Anthropologist*, 1964, 66, 1007–1028.

Levine, S. A further study of infantile handling and adult avoidance learning. *Journal of Personality*, 1956, 25, 70–80.

———. The psychophysiological effects of infantile stimulation, in E. L. Bliss, ed., *Roots of behavior*, pp. 246–253. Harper: New York, 1962.

———, G. C. Haltmeyer, G. G. Karas, & V. H. Denenberg. Physiological and behavioral effects of infantile stimulation. *Physiology and Behavior*, 1967, 2, 55–59.

Levine, S., & L. S. Otis. The effects of handling before and after weaning on the resistance of albino rats to later deprivation. *Canadian Journal of Psychology*, 1958, 12, 103–108.

Mason, W. A. The effects of social restriction on the behavior of rhesus monkeys: I. Free social behavior. *Journal of Comparative Physiological Psychology*, 1960, 53, 582–589.

Melzack, R. A., & T. H. Scott. The effects of early experience on the response to pain. *Journal of Comparative Physiological Psychology*, 1957, 50, 155–161.

Mogenson, G. J., & D. J. Ehrlich. The effects of early gentling and shock on growth and behavior in rats. *Canadian Journal of Psychology*, 1958, 12, 165–170.

Morton, J. R. C., V. H. Denenberg, & M. X. Zarrow. Modification of sexual development through stimulation in infancy. *Endocrinology*, 1963, 72, 439–442.

Newton, G., & S. Levine, eds. *Early experience and behavior*. Springfield, Ill.: Thomas, 1968.

Schaefer, T., Jr. Early "experience" and its effects on later behavioral processes in rats: II. A critical factor in the early handling phenomenon. *Transactions of the New York Academy of Sciences*, 1963, 25, 871–889.

Scott, J. H. Some effects at maturity of gentling, ignoring, or shocking rats during infancy. *Journal of Abnormal and Social Psychology*, 1955, 51, 412–414.

Scott, J. P. Critical periods in the development of social behavior in puppies. *Psychosomatic Medicine*, 1958, 20, 42–54.

———. Critical periods in behavioral development. *Science*, 1962, 138, 949–958.

———, & M. V. Marston. Critical periods affecting the development of normal and maladjustive social behavior in puppies. *Journal of Genetic Psychology*, 1950, 77, 25–60.

Seay, B., B. K. Alexander, & H. F. Harlow. Maternal behavior of socially deprived rhesus monkeys. *Journal of Abnormal and Social Psychology*, 1964, 69, 345–354.

Tryon, R. C. Genetic differences in maze-learning ability in rats. *39th Yearbook, National Society for the Study of Education*, Pt. I, 1940, pp. 111–119.

Weininger, O. The effects of early experience on behavior and growth characteristics. *Journal of Comparative Physiological Psychology*, 1956, 49, 1–9.

Whimbey, A. E., & V. H. Denenberg. Programming life histories: Creating individual differences by the experimental control of early experiences. *Multivariate Behavioral Research*, 1966, 1, 279–286.

———. Experimental programming of life histories: The factor structure underlying experimentally created individual differences. *Behaviour*, 1967, 29, 296–314.

Whiting, J. W. M. Menarcheal age and infant stress in humans, in F. A. Beach, ed., *Sex and behavior*, pp. 221–233. New York: Wiley, 1965.

———, T. K. Landauer, & T. M. Jones. Infantile immunization and adult stature. *Child Development*, 1968, 39, 58–67.

45

◈ WENDELL E. JEFFREY ◈

Early Stimulation and Cognitive Development

NOT too many years ago, the word *experience* was foreign to the professional vocabularies of most of us. I can remember my amusement, in selecting a text for my first introductory course, when I discovered that a popular textbook, from which I had been carefully protected as a student, defined psychology as the study of behavior and experience. How ridiculous! In the psychology of the day we needed to concern ourselves only with behavior, and that only within a learning model. There was no way to conceptualize a lasting effect of stimulation unless a response occurred.

Such a position was not absurd at the time, but over the years the threat of absurdity has forced considerable expansion in what we are now likely to label a response. Indeed, the history of behaviorism is epitomized by a progressive relaxation of its most basic tenets. The term *neobehaviorism* served to denote a liberalization of the concepts one was allowed to consider, the most notable of which was implicit responses as mediators of behavior. Now, some twenty years later, it is obvious that additional compromises are necessary. We can no longer question whether we should, or can, make changes; they are already with us. It is more important to consider how we can broaden our view without negating too many principles of demonstrated value.

Although this is neither the time nor the place for extensive comments

NOTE: This work was supported in part by the University of California Committee on Research and by grant MH-6639 from the United States Public Health Service.

I am grateful to my colleagues Kent Dallet and Tom Trabasso and to my students Marshall Haith, Leslie Cohen, Rochel Gelman, Katherine Nelson, and Tamar Zelniker, who have contributed in various ways to the ideas expressed in this paper, but who should not be held responsible for the final form they have taken.

about the philosophy of science, I do want to suggest that for many of us, adequate methodology has been too frequently identified with a particular model of behavior change, such as learning, and indeed with a peripheralistic interpretation of that. Although such a position is roundly endorsed by the arbiters of all that is good and holy, and one can be assured publication in establishment journals by following a few relatively simple rules, there are other cogent issues to which we must address ourselves. Many of our observations indicate that there is much more happening in most behavioral situations than current theories take into account. The fact that these theories, with admirably few parameters, can predict group behavior may be impressive to those who like playing games. They are largely inadequate, however, for the broader task at hand. Psychologists have been very ingenious at creating situations in which human beings behave like rats, but we have been much less successful at explaining why the human animal behaves so differently from rats most of the time. Indeed, we can account for the rat's behavior only under relatively restricted conditions, and the behavior of various subhuman primates causes us no end of difficulty.

There is room for both greater speculation and more empiricism without compromising well-established standards for either the conduct or the interpretation of experiments. Therefore, I want to discuss some notions regarding early stimulation and cognitive development that come from preliminary observations, but that may be provocative for the guidance of future research and theory construction.

The Effects of Early Stimulation

Current interest in the effect of early stimulus exposure on later behavior seems to be due largely to Hebb (1949), although the contributions of others, particularly ethologists, have also been very important. The overwhelming majority of the research of this sort in which psychologists have participated has been concerned primarily with changes of an affective or motivational nature (for an excellent example of such research, see Denenberg's chapter above). A few studies have also been concerned with perceptual or cognitive consequences of early stimulus exposure, and it is on these that I wish to concentrate.

It has become very popular to assume that an enriched environment has a positive effect on cognitive development and that learning alone cannot account for the tremendous growth of cognitive and language skills that is observed in the young child (Miller, 1965). No one, however, has proposed any reasonably satisfactory way of accounting for development without learning, and, more specifically to my present interest, no one has suggested how exposure to stimuli could modify the organism so as to have specific effects on later behavior.

There has been amazingly little research on this issue with either animals or men. The best studies have been done with rats and can be divided into two types. One type is concerned with the effects of an enriched environment on a generalized test of performance such as the Hebb-Williams maze. The results are typically positive (Forgays & Forgays, 1952; Forgus, 1954; Rosenzweig, 1966). Of greater interest are studies that are concerned with exposure to specific stimuli and the effects of this exposure on later problem-solving behavior using the same or similar cues (Forgus, 1955; 1958; Gibson, Walk, Pick, & Tighe, 1958). The results of these experiments also conclusively favor the experienced groups. In one of these experiments, triangular and circular forms were suspended outside the cage of the rats from the time they were two to three days of age until they reached ninety days of age. The rats were then placed in a Grice-type discrimination box to learn a triangle-circle discrimination. Positive transfer was clearly demonstrated when the exposed group was compared with a nonexposed control group. Furthermore, the positive transfer was shown to be attributable to the experience with the forms rather than to a more general increase in attending responses. A second experiment was done in order to control for this latter possibility. A group of animals that was exposed to some relatively nonspecific stimuli (rocks hung on the sides of the cages) did not show transfer. Thus, these data indicate that early exposure of the rats to triangles and circles altered or refined their perception of these forms. Although such changes are frequently identified as perceptual learning, it is difficult to suggest how any differential conditioning might have taken place in the experiment just cited. One can question whether we should call it learning when we can identify neither a response nor a reinforcer. Furthermore, what do we gain by calling it learning? It is probable that we speak of perceptual learning in order to note that the perception resulted from interaction with the environment as opposed to being innate. Only Hebb (1949) has been very precise about what occurs during early stimulus exposure, and, although he refers to perceptual learning, his notions of the development of cell assemblies and phase sequences can be considered learning only in the broadest sense of the term. It is not very profitable to quibble about how broadly we define *learning*, but I do think it is important to relieve past constraints as we concern ourselves with an adequate mechanism to integrate the facts of perceptual and cognitive development. Learning theory may account very adequately for how percepts are put to use but not for how they develop. Furthermore, even though percepts may often be seen to develop in learning situations, this does not necessarily mean that they are a product of learning.

My own ideas about what might be happening were very much influenced by an observation reported by Eleanor Gibson (1963, p. 14). In carrying out Gibson et al.'s series of experiments with rats (1958), she noted that there were inconsistencies in the results. Transfer did not always occur from early exposure to triangles and circles. This inconsistency was finally found to be attributable to the manner in which the stimuli were presented in the exposure period. In some of the studies, cutout triangles were hung on the sides of the cages, whereas in others the triangles were painted on flat backgrounds that were placed next to the cages. Although the transfer-test situation also used figures painted on flat surfaces, transfer was found to occur only if the early exposure had been to cutout stimuli. To explain this finding, Gibson reasoned that "objects having depth-at-an-edge are easily differentiated from their surroundings," and "that they are therefore noticed by the animal." This does not say why they were easily differentiated, but a reasonable guess is that depth-at-an-edge gives rise to motion parallax, and motion is a very salient cue for most organisms. Given the differentiated motion coincident with an edge, animals should attend more to the stimuli around the edge and in turn to the edge itself. It is recognized that to attribute the organism's observing behavior to motion parallax pushes the explanation back only one step, but this is an important step for it points toward the identification of those stimuli that are most influential in controlling observing behavior. However, even though motion parallax might cause the rat to attend to the stimulus repeatedly, attention to an edge, and to what it reveals and conceals, can hardly provide for the differentiation of the forms themselves required for perceptual development. Therefore, the identification of a response to an edge alone is hardly sufficient to account for the facilitation of later pattern perception, but it does suggest an approach.

Perceptual Development in the Human Infant

I shall now consider some relevant data for the human infant on which to base a model for perceptual and cognitive development from early stimulus exposure. My own interest in the perceptual development of the human infant grew out of a discrepancy: the results of observations and experiments indicated that four- to five-year-old children frequently had great difficulty in certain problem-solving situations, even though the cues could be demonstrated to be discriminable in early infancy. After establishing that many of the older children's difficulties were attributable to methodological artifacts, resulting primarily from the failure of experimenters to be concerned with the problem of controlling the children's attention, I turned to the infant in order to investigate the variables controlling attention and with the hope of looking at perceptual development at its inception.

About this same time Fantz (1958) published some startling data which additionally challenged my preconceptions about human behavior. As a better ethologist than psychologist, Fantz apparently did not know how ridiculous it was to think that an infant might show preference for one stimulus over another in the absence of previous differential conditioning. Therefore, he proceeded to test the discriminative capacity of infants by showing that they would attend more to one stimulus than another regardless of its position. The fact that he found clear differences in infants' stimulus preferences suggested that it would be profitable to investigate the degree to which the observing behavior of infants could be controlled through the manipulation of visual stimuli. Inasmuch as Haith (1966) had established that movement was a salient stimulus, we constructed some discs with segments of varying brightness and color, and mounted these on color wheel motors that could be run at a relatively slow speed. We assumed that the discs would provide stimulation of considerable salience. Papoušek (1961) had shown that head turning was under fairly good control even in the very young infant, so this was chosen as a response. Two- to six-month-old infants were placed in an infant seat located such that the two revolving discs were about four feet in front of the infant and approximately 20° to the left and right of his midline. Through the use of electronic interval timers, we could control the cycling of the wheels and, in turn, the head movements of the infant. This control was effective for varying periods, depending chiefly on the temporal parameters of stimulus presentation. For example, if the alternation between stimuli was too slow, the child would begin to fuss very early, but even with the optimal rate the infant spent less and less time observing the color wheels. If he did not start fussing, he began looking at his feet, his hands, or the ventilator in the ceiling.

Many of the infants were very distractible in this situation, and the manner in which some of them appeared to cross-check between moving and non-moving stimuli was suggestive of temporal conditioning or possibly superstitious behavior. This observation led us to design some studies within this general situation that followed both classical and operant conditioning paradigms. It is not important to describe these in detail but only to report that pseudo-conditioning occurred readily in the classical conditioning situation and furthermore that it was difficult to demonstrate anything other than pseudo-conditioning. It is not necessary, however, to demonstrate conditioning but only to establish the extent to which the observing or attending behavior of infants can be controlled by external stimulation.

Our attempts at operant conditioning of head turning toward a stationary wheel, by making the spinning of the second wheel contingent upon such a turn, produced only marginal results. Specifically, there were runs of responses that appeared to be conditioning, but then head turning would suddenly cease. It was as though the response-reinforcement contingency was being stored in short-term memory, and anything that interrupted the sequence essentially reset the system to zero. Watson (1967) has described similar results. More recently, however, Rose Caron (1967) has reported greater success at operant conditioning of head turning in a rather similar situation. She was able to increase the frequency of head turning away from the source of the reinforcing stimulus by presenting visually attractive stimuli as reinforcement. She used a variety of different stimuli in order to minimize habituation, and her training was carried out over two or more days. Thus, interesting stimuli can exert considerable influence on behavior.

A second important aspect of our own observations was the phenomenon of habituation. Various people are uneasy with this term and have substituted such rubrics as "stimulus familiarization" or "response decrement." These are admirably noncommittal descriptive terms, but I prefer to speak specifically of habituation because I do wish to implicate a process that includes not only the tendency for a stimulus to evoke a decrease in response with exposure to the stimulus but also the other attributes of habituation such as recovery and dishabituation (see Thompson & Spencer, 1966).

Unfortunately, most of the research that at first appears relevant does not include sufficiently adequate controls to permit one to say precisely that habituation has occurred, thus making the vaguer terms very appropriate. There are, nevertheless, some relevant data. Cohen (1966), for example, found that the fixation time on an array of blinking lights did habituate over trials. His study included a control group that was kept in the experimental situation for the same amount of time as the experimental group, but without stimulation from the blinking lights. When the lights were introduced at the end of the period, however, this group performed at the same level as the experimental group did at the beginning of the session. Therefore, it could be concluded that the response decrement was not due to time in the experimental situation but was related to the amount of exposure to the lights. Unfortunately, Cohen did not obtain data from a group that was habituated to, say eight lights, and then presented with four lights, and vice versa. This would have been of particular interest for the question of dishabituation. Data on dishabituation are hard to come by, and what data exist are equivocal. Nevertheless, both Bronshtein and Petrova (1967) and Bridger (1961) report some evidence for dishabituation with changes in tonal frequency; Engen, Lipsitt, and Kaye (1963) found dishabituation with changes in odors; Saayman, Ames, and Moffet (1964) obtained it with changes in visual stimuli.

There is definitely a need for more systematic data on this topic. From what exists, however, it is reasonable to conclude that habituation does occur under certain conditions and that it represents a sensory phenomenon that may be selective and that will show the properties of dishabituation and recovery. An additional and related phenomenon of interest is that there are changes in the rate of habituation with age (Cohen, 1966; Lewis, 1967).

On the basis of the data available, then, I believe the following assertions are reasonable: (a) the attention of the infant is under control of both external and internal stimulation; (b) some stimuli are more compelling or salient than others; (c) with repeated or continuous presence of the stimuli, there will be a reduction in the probability of attending, or in amount of attending, to at least all but the strongest stimuli; (d) habituation rates are a function of a number of stimulus parameters, past experience with habituation, and age.

If these testable assertions prove to be true, then they suggest a way to account for the effects of stimulus exposure on the perceptual development of infants during what appears to be a period of relatively passive exploratory behavior.

The Serial Habituation Hypothesis

As the newborn infant arrives in a visually rich environment, his gaze is captured by specific stimuli. It is unlikely that there is much habituation during the first few days, or even the first week. The lack of muscular control plus great instability in his state of arousal permits responses to a series of stimuli, and it is not necessary to attribute response variability to habituation. As the infant gains in muscular control, sustains longer periods of wakefulness, and outgrows some of his primitive postural reflexes, it is likely that environmental stimuli become increasingly dominant in their regulation of observing behavior and that variability in observing behavior becomes increasingly attributable to habituation. That is, the infant no longer fixates on a stimulus until he falls asleep or is released by a wobbly neck; for variability to occur now, the attending response to the most salient cue must habituate sufficiently so that his attention is captured by a nearby cue, the salience of which at least momentarily exceeds that of the previously dominant cue. A striking feature at this age is the degree to which attention does appear to be obligatory. However, with further exposure and, probably, additional maturation, the infant shows even quicker habituation and an observer notes that attending responses to various cues begin to occur in increasingly rapid succession.

A brief exercise, requiring rather minimal assumptions, indicates how simply one might account for the development of systematic scanning behavior on the basis of the few principles proposed. The three numerals at the top of the figure on page 54 represent the maximal relative saliencies of three cues in a stimulus complex, and the organism can respond to only one of these at a time. With each observation, the cue loses three points in strength, but with each observation of another cue, the previously observed cue recovers one point of strength. In case of ties, the cue that has not been responded to for the longest time will be chosen. It can be seen in the figure that very systematic observing behavior will occur. Note that initially there is prolonged observation of the most salient cue, followed at first by oscillation between only two cues and then inclusion of the third cue. An extension of this figure would show complete habituation to the

Cue 1	Cue 2	Cue 3	Cue 1	Cue 2	Cue 3
20	16	12	12	10	10
17	16	12	9	11	11
14	16	12	10	12	8
15	13	12	11	9	9
12	14	12	8	10	10
13	11	12	9	11	7
10	12	12	10	8	8
11	13	9	7	9	9

Systematic scanning of a stimulus complex. The salience of each component cue in a stimulus complex is represented by three arbitrarily chosen numbers. Three points are subtracted with attention to each one, and one point is added as the organism attends to another cue. When two or more cues have equal strength, attention is presumed to occur to the least observed cue.

total stimulus complex. With different parameters, however, or if there were a fourth cue in the complex, the scanning behavior would stabilize at some point and no additional habituation would take place.

If we assumed a negatively accelerated, rather than a linear, habituation function, we should find that the pattern of scanning would occur so quickly after prolonged habituation that the three cues would be observed in almost a single glance. I do not wish to propose that the simple operations that generated the figure provide an adequate mathematical model for this activity, but only to demonstrate the reasonableness of the assumption that some such activity takes place. Given some such invariants in the scanning process, then one would expect a neurological record of them. Habituation must represent some alteration of the nervous system. Hebb (1949) made some interesting speculations regarding the neurological changes involved in perceptual learning, but they have been difficult to test directly, and there has been an unfortunate dearth of alternative proposals. Nevertheless, even though speculations at the neurophysiological level do not contribute much to predictions at the level of analysis with which I am most concerned, I am convinced that the more adequate our behavior models, the more isomorphic they will be with the neurological models that finally develop. Therefore, the fact that the twain do not conveniently meet at this time should not retard our speculations at the behavioral level, nor discourage us from keeping the neurophysiology of the situation in mind.

Behavioral data lead to the undeniable conclusion that humans do come to recognize objects as such during infancy. Research by Piaget (1954) and Charlesworth (1966) shows that object percepts as indicated by concepts of object permanence are present as early as eight months of age. It is also true that objects present certain invariant relations, and these must in some way represent at least part of what is involved in object perception (Gibson, 1966). Although the model presented in the figure suggests that orderly scanning would take place, it is not necessary that this be the case, for the perceptual response is not the scanning activity itself. In tactual perception, one does not have to feel the attributes of a complex stimulus in any particular order to recognize what it is. Furthermore, as Gibson points out, visual perception is similar to tactual perception in that, contrary to the camera analogy, what is perceived visually is a construction from successive glances and past experiences and thus, although it is built up by scanning, the resultant percept is not the scanning activity itself. If one considers audition, it should also be obvious that perception cannot be accounted for by motor responses. Nevertheless, the serial habituation model can be equally easily applied to auditory perception (Jeffrey, 1968).

Returning to visual object perception, an additional step beyond what has already been indicated would appear to be necessary. That is, not only must the infant scan the invariants of objects — the corners, edges, texture, and so forth — but he must attend to the interface between the object and its surround. With slight head movements, the object on which he has focused will move in a direction contrary to aspects of the background. This movement has attention value or salience, and it is also an aid to, if not indispensable to, the development of object perception because it frequently represents the termination of a cluster of invariants. There will be no single additional feature of the environment that always accompanies the features of the object except motion parallax. Therefore, I propose that both the scanning within the object's borders and the separation of the object from its surround are necessary for the development of an object percept.

It is possible that object percepts that are developed first are those that occur in a highly variable but undistracting context. High variability would help to isolate the invariant properties of the object from its background, yet background cues should not be so salient as to disrupt the infant's scanning of less salient cues within an object. This analysis also implies that the perception of depth is a likely concomitant of the development of object perception. The salience of the cues indicating the disjunction between one object percept and the rest of the environment is likely to cause this additional, more abstract invariant to be explored as the infant peruses his surroundings. It could be that perception of depth is the earliest preoccupation of the infant and, as previously suggested, that motion parallax could account for the differential effects of exposure to cutout versus painted figures in the studies by Gibson et al. It should be noted, however, that once the rats had had experience with the cutout stimuli, transfer occurred for stimuli presented in only two dimensions. Thus, the attention-getting value of the edge and motion parallax may be required to form the original percept, but once the percept is formed, the object can be identified in a two-dimensional representation. The difficulty that monkeys and young children have in using dimensional cues in problem-solving situations occurs at a sufficiently older age to suggest that it is probably due to poor cue salience rather than to the subjects' not having formed the appropriate perceptual structures.

Given that the infant perceives objects in space, we can also conceptualize additional refinements of perception. First, it should be noted that in speaking of eye fixations we are dealing with a molar concept. The photographs by Salapatek and Kessen (1966) of an infant attending to a triangle, as well as observations of my own, show that there are many saccadic micro-adjustments interspersed with the grosser movements that might go from one corner to another or from object to object. Fixation times as typically reported obviously represent the times between these gross adjustments. It is likely that with increased experience there is an acceleration of this complex scanning process and that, as perceptual structures are formed, some of the attending responses may drop out. Just as we take in the wall in front of us with only a few cursory glances, we may also recognize a cube on the basis of a configuration of angles and a side. Given the juxtaposition of a cube and a pyramid, as the infant looks from one to the other, the second will not fit the construction generated by the first in any of its various transformations. That such discrepancies become salient cues is a generally accepted but little understood phenomenon. Sokolov (1963) assumes that the orienting reflex is aroused when an input is discrepant from a neurological model that has been established as the result of earlier observations. Berlyne (1960) suggests that stimulus discrepancy, or novel stimulation, induces a conflict and that the organism attends in order to reduce his conflict. Whatever the cause, additional observations occur that provide for further development of the percepts involved. I submit that such alterations of perception continue throughout adulthood in this very manner. Although some of these refinements may result from problem-solving demands or tuition, many are primarily a function of exposure to stimulation. That is, although we may be taught to count corners, compare angles, and so forth, in the context of solving a problem, many natural situations arise where perceptual changes occur without external demands being placed on the person. For example, I am convinced that one's appreciation of differences among wines improves with experience even without tuition, and that the major contribution of tuition in this instance is the opportunity for immediate comparison.

The Development of Abstractions

Comparison is obviously an important aspect of the formation of abstract percepts, as can be seen in the perception of color. One suspects that color is a very salient cue, particularly in early infancy, yet there are considerable data that suggest it is not used readily in problem-solving situations even as late as four years of age, particularly if other cues are available. There is also evidence of difficulty in learning color names, though it seems apparent that the child is capable of discriminating the colors themselves. The data, however, are ambiguous and difficult to interpret. I suspect that a particularly sensitive test of the infant's basic potential for discriminating colors could be obtained by using the optokinetic reflex with moving bands of differing colors of equal brightness in place of the black and white stripes frequently used for tests of visual acuity during infancy. One might also habituate some autonomic response to the onset of one color, and test for dishabituation by presenting a light of a different color. If either of these tests indicated that infants could respond differentially to differing wavelengths of light, then the failure of the infant to use color cues would probably reflect the fact that such cues are of infrequent help in most problem-solving situations, at least at early ages. It should also be noted that in spite of a few play objects that may differ only in color, for the majority of objects in everyday life, color is one of the invariant attributes of the object. Therefore, during the very early period when color and brightness may dominate attention, color would not necessarily be separated from object percepts, as would size, until the infant has some prolonged experience with objects that are identical except for color. Thus, it is important to distinguish between being able to respond to

57

color as part of a cue complex and to use it as an abstract attribute while ignoring other features of an object.

Abstracting an object percept from the size differences that arise with varying distances between the observer and the object may be relatively easy because of the pervasiveness of size changes as well as because the perception of depth develops very early (Bower, 1966; Walk & Gibson, 1961). It is also of interest, however, that for animals at least, the variable features of proximal cues tend to make them less likely to be used in problem-solving situations than background cues of greater stability (Neisser, 1967).

As the infant develops object percepts that are independent of size or color, eventually he must also become aware of differences in the sizes of objects when they lie in the same plane. As higher levels of form differentiation grow out of comparison situations, so must the perception of size. This will happen, however, only when attending responses to the forms themselves are fairly well habituated. It is for this reason that perceptions involving relationships are likely to be developed later than the less abstract object percepts. Abstractness, I suggest, is highly correlated with the number of salient cues to which the organism must habituate before he attends to the cues in question. Once he does attend to the appropriate cues, such as those involved in a size discrimination, his attention is caught again by an invariant relationship that must result in a structure that in this instance is a recognition of inequality in height. For these cues to be used in problem-solving, they must be as salient as the various features of the objects once were, and this may take some time. However, it is also important to keep in mind that there is room for considerable discrepancy between the ability to perceive size differences and the ability to respond on the basis of a size relationship in a test of transposition. The latter is not a test of whether a child *can* respond to a size relationship but only of whether he *does* respond to the relationship under a certain set of conditions. The infant, of course, can respond to size without having to come to grips with the concept of relative size.

So far, I have suggested that most early perceptual or cognitive development occurs in an essentially passive organism. In general, he need move no more than his eyes and his head, and the latter only slightly in most instances. I should not wish to minimize for a minute, however, the important contribution of such activities as reaching, climbing, handling, and touching as aids in delineating and elaborating perception. We must also recognize that the saliency of cues may be markedly modified by their association with pain avoidance, food, mother's approval, and so forth. Nevertheless, the child is continuously responding to his environment, and it is not necessary for him to be engaged in some type of problem-solving activity in order for the nervous system to be altered.

I was particularly impressed recently by a video tape made by Marshall Haith. With the use of a special infrared-sensitive vidicon tube and infrared light, he was able to observe and record the activities of an infant in complete darkness. The eyes of one infant were seen to be actively exploring, or possibly it is more appropriate to say searching, a non-visible environment. It is impossible to say what was controlling this behavior, of course. He may have been hallucinating or observing an eidetic image. On the basis of other observations, however, it is equally reasonable to assume that the nervous system is set up to monitor the environment continuously, even in the absence of salient external cues and regardless of its state of arousal, which may control only the level of monitoring activities. Inasmuch as we have evidence that organisms do to tend to seek stimulation, under reduced stimulation you might expect either that an infant would be more highly active or that the nervous system would adjust itself to operate at a different level — that is, to sleep, which is also a frequent consequence of reduced stimulation. Nevertheless, a certain amount of scanning activity apparently occurs even during sleep, for the selective attention of which sleeping adults are shown to be capable suggests that this is the case.

Critical Hypotheses and Supporting Data

Cognitive behavior becomes exceedingly complex very early in life. Before I demonstrate how the model might be applied to some of the more complex cognitive phenomena of childhood, it may be appropriate to re-evaluate it in terms of a more careful analysis of some of the data on which it rests and to indicate the specific needs for additional data of a supporting nature, as well as to spell out some of the hypotheses that the model generates at this level.

First, as for the basic assumptions of the model, the differential attractiveness of stimuli is readily demonstrable, but we do not have good independent measures of the dimensions that appear to be important. Although it will be valuable to work out some of these relationships in greater detail, we have done very well in research on learning with only a response-inferred definition of our most critical variable — reinforcement — and we may have to be content to rely on similarly circular definitions with regard to stimulus salience. A particularly difficult problem arises because relevant dimensions such as complexity and novelty must be referred to the subject's experience with the stimuli and therefore their salience is ever changing. If one accepts Sokolov's (1963) definition of the orienting reflex as a pattern of physiological responses, it is possible to scale stimuli with these measures and then to make predictions regarding other attending behaviors, but, unfortunately, these physiological responses too frequently provide our only measures of attention.

More critical is the need for additional data on habituation. Current data are somewhat conflicting, primarily, I believe, as a result of the lack of systematic research. For the most part, people have not set out to study the parameters of habituation or even to demonstrate it as such, but rather have noticed only its presence or absence or have used it as a tool to demonstrate discriminative ability. To know the parameters of habituation, dishabituation, and recovery is an important first step before we should speculate too much about what takes place with repeated exposure. Sokolov's notion that habituation occurs with the construction of a neurological model is appealing, but it says very little. I and others have spoken of the development of schemata, but that term is used so broadly at times as to be meaningless in general, and for the task at hand it says no more than "neurological model," "percept," or "cognitive structure." I think it is reasonable and heuristic to search for some way of conceptualizing what may be occurring inside the organism, but naming is not going to help by itself. Studies of cross-modal transfer are particularly attractive with regard to the ideas they suggest about cognitive structures, and I look forward to increasing activity in this area. For other speculations regarding what might be inside, I strongly recommend Gibson's (1966) *The Senses Considered as Perceptual Systems* and Neisser's (1967) *Cognitive Psychology*. As more people confront the basic issues of perception and memory with refined or new approaches, we are bound to make progress. To be uncomfortably vague about what may be taking place inside the organism leaves us in no worse condition than to be terribly precise, if all we put in is an S-R bond.

Although research that relates to the foundations of a model is important, the real utility of the model rests in what it says that may be relevant to our general goals. I shall comment first on what the model at its simplest level might imply and then indicate how it also accounts for some of the more complex problem-solving behaviors in childhood.

I have already noted that the model does agree with the common sense notion that early stimulation will affect cognitive development. It would be more important if it specified what stimulus events should occur and the order in which they should occur, but that is asking too much at the moment. More data, however, should begin to make such statements possible. The model does suggest that a few simple objects in a relatively uncluttered surrounding would be more likely to produce early object perception than would a stimulus situation that is overloaded with cues of high salience. On the other hand, we do not know whether the effect of being bombarded with high salience cues may be of special use in providing the infant with exercise in the control of his receptors and whether this may also be a necessary forerunner of any more precise perceptual development. Resolving this question, then, would be an important first step toward formulating more specific hypotheses. Certainly at later stages the former principle — placing a few salient cues in a relatively impoverished environment — will facilitate cue-selection behavior in most problem-solving situations. If the child is not responding to the appropriate cue, one can combine a highly salient cue with one of low salience and otherwise reduce the number of cues in the surround such that as the child habituates to the more salient cue only the previously unnoticed cue remains. This operation is accomplished even more effectively by fading the more salient cue. Fading makes it possible to continue to use reinforcement to maintain both interest in the situation and attention to the cue complex, whereas habituation frequently requires prolonged absence of reinforcement during which the subject may lose all interest in the situation.

It may be appropriate to comment again about learning in the context of this model. Reinforcement has the function of retarding habituation. Therefore, given attention to appropriate cues during response-contingent reinforcement, it would appear that the relevant associations are made quickly and with little difficulty. I propose that most learning situations of a problem-solving or instrumental nature require a number of trials because of the time it takes to habituate attention to the irrelevant cues or stimulus dimensions. We are mistaken to think that increased stimulus-complexity prolongs learning; it only delays the discovery of the critical cue, and it does that only if the critical cue is of lesser salience than the other cues involved. The process of forming associations is probably not

61

prolonged. Thus, any activity or pretraining that assures appropriate attending responses, such as learning-set training, or training that otherwise assures rapid habituation to the irrelevant cues, will result in rapid problem-solving.

The Role of Language in Cognitive Development

When considering most problem-solving activities with children of two and a half to three years of age and older, one frequently becomes concerned with the role played by language. Although we have taken great care not to anthropomorphize with animal subjects, we have rightfully been confused with regard to children. We did everything we could to demonstrate that their behavior did not differ from that of rats, but when it did differ, we immediately attributed the difference to language. As adults, we are so dependent on language and so skillful in translating percepts, images, and memories into language that we cannot help believing that language is indispensable to cognitive behavior. With respect to the period from two to five years of age, and contrary to the acquired-distinctiveness of cues hypothesis (Miller, 1948), I have never been able to see how the addition of a label would aid in a discrimination unless the label carried with it some means of directing attention — that is, had some meaning or could be used for purposes of rehearsal during the absence of a stimulus (Spiker, 1960). I submit that labeling does not aid discrimination learning — that words acquire meaning or utility only when attached to a percept or concept and that this attachment takes place only after a percept is formed. Brown (1958) proposed some time ago that the application of labels to schemata is the original word game. The child does find it interesting to discover that names can be applied to objects, and, indeed, I presume that nouns are learned first because object percepts are developed first. Thus, to indicate to the child that "this is a cow" and "this is a horse" may be useful in maintaining the child's attention to the two relevant stimuli. However, the labels can be attached only to differential percepts, and because these percepts will come only from continued observation, they could be brought about by other means than labeling. Names for more abstract concepts will be learned only after the more abstract concepts are formed — and this, in turn, can occur only after percepts are formed for the irrelevant aspects of an instance of an abstract concept, and then attending responses are habituated to these percepts. Thus, the richer

62

the early cognitive experience, the earlier the child should be able to form abstract concepts.

It is possible that if labels are to be useful, they would be most useful in facilitating habituation to component percepts, by indicating what cues should be ignored. An active rather than a passive process of cue elimination may even be essential for the elaboration of highly abstract concepts. Nevertheless, it should be emphasized that the "insight" that appears to be contiguous with the application of a label is a function not of the labeling but of the formation of a structure representing the concept to which the label or any other response can finally be reliably attached.

Conservation

Training on very abstract concepts, such as conservation of quantity or mass, is frequently shown to have been unsuccessful when a generalized test is given. It is often the case that the training is inadequate because it was not properly devised to inhibit or habituate attention to the more salient perceptual cues. Gelman (1967) found that by using a variation of the learning-set technique, she obtained evidence of conservation in five-year-old children and in addition found transfer to a generalized test. The essence of the learning-set technique is, of course, the accelerated habituation of responses to irrelevant cues, and there can be little question of its effectiveness. It remains possible, however, that even with highly adequate training, there will still be some failures on generalized tests for the attainment of a concept. I see two reasons for this. First, children neither understand nor listen to instructions very well, and second, their activity is more strongly guided by the desire to interact with the situation than it is by the need for either the approval of the experimenter or the receipt of a token reinforcer. Thus, they meet each new situation with an impetuosity that makes them more likely to respond to the immediate perceptual cues than to the more abstract conceptual cues regardless of instructions. There is an additional difficulty. Conservation problems direct the child to answer a question of sameness or difference. The fact that this question is very difficult for children even when relatively simple and obvious cues are involved is a provocative one that needs investigation.

Even if the child does understand sameness and difference there is an additional problem with the standard conservation experiment. The experimental procedure strongly suggests that the child should look at the cues presented in order to answer the experimenter's question. Yet the only proper basis for a correct solution comes not from looking at the perceptual cues, or even from trying to make judgments regarding compensating changes, but from having learned that mass, for example, is invariant regardless of form as long as nothing is added or taken away. In a similar type of problem, Bruner and Kenney (1966) found that children were unable to judge the relative fullness of two tumblers differing in height because they apparently responded only to the absolute levels involved. We found that they had little difficulty, however, if they were given first the experience of judging whether some glasses were half full, more than half full, or less than half full. From their performance on twelve such pretraining trials, it was clear that they did not have to learn this task. They could already perform it, and once their attention was drawn to the dimension of fullness, they no longer attended to absolute differences in the original test situation but only to the proportions. It is in this manner that many of our test situations mislead us regarding the conceptual development of children — the child may be misled, or at least not properly informed, with regard to the solution of the problem. Therefore, although the failure of children to perform according to our expectations in such situations may indeed indicate differences in developmental level, specific implications of these studies for the presence or absence of cognitive structures must be interpreted with caution.

Discussion

I have attempted to keep the model as simple as possible but at the same time to show that the basic ideas have considerable scope. I hope that my hop, skip, and jump across cognitive development from birth to middle childhood has not been too confusing.

First, some specific notes on the terminology I have used. I avoided using the term *orienting reflex* because it generates considerable confusion among people who may not be aware of Sokolov's definition, and even when such a definition is accepted and understood, the relation between the orienting reflex and attention is not very clear. *Attention* is probably too broad a term and covers too much ground, but I think that as we get used to using it and thinking in terms of what it suggests, we shall gain a better understanding of all that must be involved. It is important to note that although measures of attention are typically peripheral, I am concerned in the end with a central event of a selective nature. We have a long way to go before we understand what is involved in attention, but continued work such as that presented in Maccoby's chapter will most certainly be helpful.

I have also avoided another term that has become very popular, the *schema*. I, too, have found it appealing in the past (Jeffrey, 1968), but I find now that it is used so broadly by some that it loses most of its utility. Therefore, it seemed preferable to stick with some classic terms such as *percept* and *concept* to refer to some of the internal processes that determine future reactions, whatever their ultimate representation. Having done this, it may be appropriate to relegate the word *schema* to some of its broader uses — specifically, to symbolize relations among percepts and concepts.

I have de-emphasized learning as a variable in cognitive development primarily to make the alternative point — that perceptual development can and does take place outside the classical learning paradigms, at least as they are most rigidly interpreted. Nevertheless, I strongly believe that learning situations frequently set the occasion for the occurrence of perceptual and conceptual development and that if one wishes to facilitate cognitive development, particularly after the first year of life, it would be well to manipulate stimuli in order to give them ecological significance.

Lastly, I wish to re-emphasize the importance of considering the human organism as a continuously active system. Innate and developmental factors interact with the amount and type of stimulation the infant receives to determine the direction the activity takes and to effect orderly changes in neural activity. Inasmuch as these changes take place under specifiable conditions, our task is to establish the parameters of these conditions. In contrast to some investigators, I think such speculation is valuable if it suggests new and interesting ways of obtaining and organizing information about these parameters.

References

Berlyne, D. E. *Conflict, arousal, and curiosity.* New York: McGraw-Hill, 1960.

Bower, T. G. R. The visual world of infants. *Scientific American,* 1966, 215, 80–92.

Bridger, W. H. Sensory habituation and discrimination in the human neonate. *American Journal of Psychiatry,* 1961, 117, 991–996.

Bronshtein, A. I., & E. P. Petrova. The auditory analyser in young infants, in Y. Brackbill & G. G. Thompson, eds., *Behavior in infancy and early childhood,* pp. 163–172. New York: Free Press, 1967.

Brown, R. *Words and things.* Glencoe, Ill.: Free Press, 1958.

Bruner, J. S., & H. J. Kenney. On relational concepts, in J. S. Bruner, R. R. Olver,

& P. M. Greenfield, eds., *Studies in cognitive development*. New York: Wiley, 1966.

Caron, R. F. Visual reinforcement of head-turning in young infants. *Journal of Experimental Child Psychology*, 1967, 5, 489–511.

Charlesworth, W. R. Development of the object concept: A methodological study. Paper presented at the meeting of the American Psychological Association, New York, September 1966.

Cohen, L. B. Observing responses, visual preferences and habituation to visual stimuli in infants. Ph.D. thesis, University of California, Los Angeles, 1966. Ann Arbor, Mich.: University Microfilms, 1966, No. 66-7133.

Engen, T., L. P. Lipsitt, & H. Kaye. Olfactory responses and adaptation in the human neonate. *Journal of Comparative and Physiological Psychology*, 1963, 56, 73–77.

Fantz, R. L. Pattern vision in young infants. *Psychological Record*, 1958, 8, 43–47.

Forgays, D. G., & J. W. Forgays. The nature of the effect of free-environmental experience in the rat. *Journal of Comparative and Physiological Psychology*, 1952, 45, 322–328.

Forgus, R. H. The effect of early perceptual learning on the behavioral organization of adult rats. *Journal of Comparative and Physiological Psychology*, 1954, 47, 331–336.

―――. Early visual and motor experience as determiners of complex maze-learning ability under rich and reduced stimulation. *Journal of Comparative and Physiological Psychology*, 1955, 48, 215–220.

―――. The interaction between form pre-exposure and test requirements in determining form discrimination. *Journal of Comparative and Physiological Psychology*, 1958, 51, 588–595.

Gelman, R. S. Conservation, attention and discrimination. Ph.D. thesis, University of California, Los Angeles, 1967. Ann Arbor, Mich.: University Microfilms, 1967, No. 67-16031.

Gibson, E. J. Development of perception: Discrimination of depth compared with discrimination of graphic symbols, in J. C. Wright & J. Kagan, eds., Basic cognitive processes in children. *Monographs of the Society for Research in Child Development*, 1963, 28 (2, Serial No. 86), 5–24.

―――, R. D. Walk, H. L. Pick, Jr., & T. J. Tighe. The effect of prolonged exposure to visual patterns on learning to discriminate similar and different patterns. *Journal of Comparative and Physiological Psychology*, 1958, 51, 585–595.

Gibson, J. J. *The senses considered as perceptual systems*. Boston: Houghton-Mifflin, 1966.

Haith, M. M. Response of the human newborn to movement. *Journal of Experimental Child Psychology*, 1966, 3, 225–234.

Hebb, D. O. *The organization of behavior*. New York: Wiley, 1949.

Jeffrey, W. E. The orienting reflex and attention in cognitive development. *Psychological Review*, 1968, 75, 323–334.

Lewis, M. Infant attention: Response decrement as a measure of cognitive processes, or what's new Baby Jane? Paper presented at the meeting of the Society for Research in Child Development, New York, March 1967.

Miller, G. A. Some preliminaries to psycholinguistics. *American Psychologist*, 1965, 20, 15–20.

Miller, N. E. Theory and experiment relating psychoanalytic displacement to stimulus-response generalization. *Journal of Abnormal and Social Psychology*, 1948, 43, 155–178.

Neisser, U. *Cognitive psychology*. New York: Appleton, 1967.

Papoušek, H. Conditioned head rotation reflexes in infants in the first months of life. *Acta Paediatrica*, 1961, 50, 565–576.

WENDELL E. JEFFREY

Piaget, J. *The construction of reality in the child.* New York: Basic Books, 1954.

Rosenzweig, M. R. Environmental complexity, cerebral changes, and behavior. *American Psychologist,* 1966, 21, 321–332.

Saayman, G., E. W. Ames, & A. Moffett. Response to novelty as an indicator of visual discrimination in the human infant. *Journal of Experimental Child Psychology,* 1964, 1, 189–198.

Salapatek, P., & W. Kessen. Visual scanning of a triangle by the human newborn. *Journal of Experimental Child Psychology,* 1966, 3, 155–167.

Sokolov, Y. N. *Perception and the conditioned reflex.* New York: Macmillan, 1963.

Spiker, C. C. Associative transfer in verbal paired associative learning. *Child Development,* 1960, 31, 73–87.

Thompson, R. F., & W. A. Spencer. Habituation: A model phenomenon for the behavior. *Psychological Review,* 1966, 73, 16–43.

Walk, R. D., & E. J. Gibson. A comparative and analytical study of visual depth perception. *Psychological Monographs,* 1961, 75, 1–44.

Watson, J. S. Memory and "Contingency analysis" in infant learning. *Merrill-Palmer Quarterly,* 1967, 13, 55–76.

◆ ELEANOR E. MACCOBY ◆

The Development of Stimulus Selection

THE problem of stimulus selection arises from the fact that there is a greater array of stimulation potentially available to an organism at any given moment than the organism can take in, remember, or respond to. I say "potentially available" because, of course, not all the stimuli which could impinge upon the sense organs in a given situation actually do so. This is especially true of vision, where the perceiver has a choice of what to look at, and may indeed choose to shut his eyes altogether and not receive any of the visual stimulation that is available.

The selective activity of the eyes can be quite finely attuned. The eyes can be used as efficient information-gathering instruments, scanning relevant contours or focusing upon the most informative portions of a display, while also gathering less precise information through peripheral vision. Stimulus selection is not accomplished entirely through the selective orientation of the receptors, however. The perceiver can modulate centrally the stimuli which have impinged upon his sense organs. That is, the same stimulus will sometimes evoke a high-amplitude excitation in the sensory projection areas of the brain, sometimes a small one, depending on the significance of the stimulus to the subject (Sutton, Tueting, Zubin, & John, 1967). Sutton et al.'s work follows and confirms the original findings of Hernandez-Peon and his colleagues, who indicated that the amplitude of impulses coming in from the sense organs of one modality was attenuated when the subject was attending to stimuli in another modality; even within a single modality, selective attention could increase the amplitude of certain portions of the stimulus field and decrease that of others (Palestini, Davidovich, & Hernandez-Peon, 1959). This regulation oc-

68

curs after the eyes have chosen what to look at, and constitutes a second means of selecting wanted stimulation.

Selection can be accomplished in still a third way. There is a time during which the given stimulus impinges directly on the sense organs. Beyond this, the effective stimulation time is increased somewhat by perseveration in the form of an image or trace. Neisser (1967) called this trace "iconic memory" in vision and "echoic memory" in audition. The trace gives the perceiver extra time in which to use or process portions of the information contained in the stimulus. Sperling (1960) has shown that for a brief period after visual stimulation — approximately half a second — the perceiver can "read" selectively from a visual image. With very brief presentation of a stimulus — so brief that there is time for only a single fixation, and no time for selective scanning with the eyes — there is then a period of time, including both the stimulation period itself and the "trace" period which follows it, during which the perceiver can select those portions of the stimulus display that are most informative or most relevant to his task. At a later point, I shall review some of the evidence that the perceiver can and does carry out selective operations at this point, in addition to the selection that is accomplished through sense-organ orientation.

There can be a difference of opinion concerning the proper definition and terminology for selection which involves a stimulus trace as well as the period of actual stimulation. Are we dealing here with selective *perception* or selective *memory*? The distinction seems an arbitrary one. There is a continuous series of processes, beginning with the orientation of the sense organs and the peripheral registration of energy at the sense organs, followed by a series of operations carried out directly upon the incoming sense data or upon the data as briefly stored. The operations include such processes as coding and the search for matching items in long-term store. *Recognition* involves the achievement of some kind of match. The term *perception* has traditionally been used in psychology to include processes much more complex than mere reception of sense data; specifically, it includes pattern recognition. Hence, I shall use the term *selective perception* to include the entire series of operations involved in recognition, with the additional proviso that there are portions of the available sense data being ignored — *not* recognized, and not responded to. The purpose of the present paper is to review a number of hypotheses concerning the development of these selective processes in childhood. We will attempt to see whether the set of hypotheses form a coherent picture, and whether existing evidence assists the choice between conflicting points of view.

Hypothesis I. With increasing age and experience, children come to orient their sense organs more efficiently, so that (a) the material which registers on the sense organs with maximum clarity is increasingly that material which carries the most information relative to the task-set of the perceiver; and (b) focusing upon the most informative material occurs more and more rapidly.

Most of the work on sense-organ orientation has been done with vision, since it is possible to observe and record the perceiver's eye movements. Some observations have also been made of the hand and finger movements by which a subject attempts to recognize something by touch.

In studies of visual orientation in newborn infants, it is not always easy to determine whether an infant is fixating on a whole visual pattern or only a selected portion of it. For example, in Fantz's work (e.g., 1961), where the infant fixates for a longer time on a bull's-eye than on a striped pattern or on a solid triangle, one cannot be sure whether the infant is fixating on just one ring, or a portion of a ring, or the whole bull's-eye. Photographs of the infant's eye movements and fixations, superimposed on a representation of the pattern he is looking at, give somewhat more detailed data. Using concurrent film records, Salapatek and Kessen (1966) presented triangles to infants under eight days of age. The infants tended to fixate a single corner of the triangle, or even a spot slightly outside the contours of the figure, but did not explore the figure with their eyes. Working with older children, Zaporozhets (1965) also photographed eye movements, finding that children under four years of age tended to fixate a given point for quite a long time instead of scanning a figure, and that what eye movements did occur were along a single central line within the figure. Four- and five-year-olds made more eye movements, but these were within the figure — the child tended to look from one end of it to the other, tracing the length or the width, but not tracing the outer contours. It was not until the age of six or seven that children would go around the outline of the figure with their eyes, dwelling on distinctive features; the development of this kind of visual scanning was associated with improved recognition of the figure when the child was asked to select it from among an array of similar figures.

Zaporozhets found a similar development of scanning with the fingers, by touch. When asked to explore a form behind a screen by touch so that they can recognize it later, very young children will simply hold it or press it; older children will trace the outline with a fingertip.

Unfortunately, there is a methodological problem with Zaporozhets's work on eye movements. The photographing was done with a camera lens centered in the visual display and clearly visible to the subject. One can only wonder whether a round shiny object, in some ways resembling a human eye, might have been more attractive to younger children than older ones, and might have kept their gaze centered, thus restricting the scanning of contours that otherwise might have occurred. Recent technological advances have made it possible to obtain a photographic record of eye movements without the camera's being in the line of sight. Using these methods, Mackworth and Bruner (1966) have compared six-year-olds with adults, finding that there are differences between these two age groups in the use of the eyes for information gathering. The pictures used as stimuli were divided into small segments, and each segment was independently rated (by a different group of subjects) on its informativeness. Then the pictures were shown to subjects whose eye movements were being photographed, and it was found that adults tend to spend proportionally more of their time looking at the most informative portions of a picture. Children concentrated their gaze successively on a few isolated points, and did not cover as much of the display. This finding did not imply, however, that adults spend more of their time tracing contours. The Mackworth-Bruner stimuli were not outline drawings of simple figures, but in-focus or out-of-focus photographs of objects (such as a fire hydrant). It is not necessarily the contours that are the most informative portions of such pictures. When the pictures were in sharp focus, there was some indication that children tended to seek edges more than adults did, as though they were operating on the assumption that contours were always the most informative elements in a display even when this was not the case.

Using the same improved techniques of eye photography, Vurpillot (1968) studied the eye movements of children ranging in age from three to nine years of age when they were asked to compare pictures of two houses and to say whether they were the same or different. The pairs of houses varied in how many of their corresponding windows differed. The most efficient search pattern would be to compare the windows pair by pair, and to stop the search as soon as a difference was found. This is the strategy the older subjects employed. The youngest subjects, on the other hand, used their eyes unsystematically, comparing non-corresponding portions of the display, and often gathering too little information to make a correct decision. There was no relation between the length of their search and the number of comparisons that were needed for an accurate performance.

There is considerable evidence, then, that Hypothesis I is true. There is improvement during childhood in the skill with which the child deploys his eye movements. If we accept Zaporozhets's work as demonstrating an increased scanning of contours with eye, and assume further that contours are the most informative portions of outline drawings of simple figures, then his work constitutes evidence for increased selection of those portions of a display which yield the most information. With more complex displays, involving gradients of texture and brightness, and having internal focal points where there is maximal complexity, the hypothesis would predict that it would be these focal points, rather than edges, that would be increasingly sought by older subjects. Although there is no research which deals with the *speed* with which children of different ages locate the most informative features of a display with their eyes, the work of Mackworth and Bruner shows that adults spend a larger portion of their fixation time on such features. It is important to be as precise as possible about what is meant by "most informative." For the present purposes, the phrase refers to those features of a display which relate to task-relevant decisions, and which are most useful in distinguishing the display (or portions of it) from other likely possibilities. In this sense, the most informative portions of a display are the same as its "distinctive features," and therefore Hypothesis I is entirely consistent with Gibson's view (e.g., 1963, p. 169) that, with further development, the child comes to attend more fully to the distinctive features of a display. To my knowledge, no one has presented children with minimal-contrast pairs of visual stimuli to see whether the eyes dwell upon the criterial feature which distinguishes them, and whether this is increasingly true as children grow older; but clearly, such a prediction would follow from Hypothesis I.

Parenthetically, it is of interest to note that the acquisition of skill in focusing upon selected features of a stimulus complex appears to be responsive to standard learning conditions. A number of experimenters have reinforced children for directing their gaze at certain portions of the stimulus field (Quay, Sprague, Werry, & McQueen, 1967; Solley & Santos, in Solley & Murphy, 1960, pp. 190ff; Witryol, 1967), and have found that visual orientation can be fairly precisely controlled by reinforcement contingencies.

HYPOTHESIS II

Hypothesis II. There is an increase with age in the ability to select a wanted stimulus out of a complex array, even when the selection cannot be accomplished by the differential orientation of the sense organs.

How does one find out whether this kind of selective perception has occurred? With respect to vision, the following procedure can be used: We can tell a subject that we are going to show him a series of pictures of objects. In successive trials, the pictures vary in the number, color, and identity of the objects displayed. We say that we shall show each picture only very briefly, and that we want him to concentrate on the color of the objects. We then show him a picture so briefly that he has time for only a single fixation; he cannot scan the picture with his eyes. Then, we ask him what color the objects were. We can contrast his performance under these conditions with performances when he was not told what to concentrate on, but is asked only *after* stimulation to report what color the objects were. If a selective set improved his performance, we have evidence that he was able to somehow "tune" himself selectively to perceive only certain portions, or certain attributes of a display.

Külpe used this method many years ago, and since Külpe's time there have been a number of studies which contrast perception based on a pre-stimulus set with perception revealed by "post-stimulus sampling." Some studies have revealed an effect of prior set, some have not, depending on a number of experimental conditions. For example, Lawrence and LaBerge (1956) reported that there was an advantage for subjects who had prior instructions, but that this advantage disappeared if one controlled for the order of report. That is, they concluded that the prior instructions affected not what the subject perceived, but only the order in which he reported what he perceived, with first-reported attributes being reported more accurately. Harris and Haber (1963) found, on the other hand, that prior instructions do permit the subject to perceive selectively, and that the effect is *not* accounted for by the order of report. Their work revealed, however, that the utility of a prior signal depends on whether the subject is coding the input by objects or dimensions. Sperling (1960) found that subjects were able to select one line from a display of several lines if they received the instruction signal either at the time of stimulation or immediately after, while the "trace" was still available. When he asked his subjects to select either numbers or letters out of a mixed array, however, he found that for most of his subjects the prior signal did not help. Broadbent recently found that prior instructions improve the selective perception of those stimuli which are all of a given color, but they do not help the subject to select letters rather than numbers. He holds that the utility of a selective set depends upon how much information processing is necessary to identify a stimulus as belonging to the chosen or excluded class.

I shall comment later on some of the possible implications of these experiments for selective processes in children. To my knowledge, there have been no studies involving post-stimulus sampling from visual displays among children of different ages. The studies as a group, then, do not bear upon the issue of developmental changes in stimulus selection. They do show that, among adults, there are complex conditions which determine whether the perceiver can set himself to select only certain portions of a briefly presented visual display. For some classes of stimuli, and under certain training conditions, he can do so. Under other experimental conditions, the primary mode of selection in vision would appear to be the selective focusing of the eyes upon those portions of the display the perceiver most wants to see.

With respect to audition, the role of receptor orientation is necessarily less than in vision, since the ears cannot be closed or oriented to shut out unwanted sounds. Hence, the work on stimulus selection in hearing falls primarily under Hypothesis II. That selection does occur is demonstrated in the work on dichotic listening, where two different messages are fed simultaneously to the two ears, and the subject is asked to "shadow" one of the messages. Under these conditions the listener can report one of the messages but not both. He can select which message to listen to on the basis of which ear it comes to; but the role of preparatory set, in comparison with post-stimulus sampling, has been little studied in audition, and it is only recently that we have had information concerning age changes in selective listening. Much of the work that my colleagues and I have done at Stanford on developmental changes in these processes has been published (Maccoby, 1967; Maccoby & Konrad, 1967). Therefore, I shall give only a few details of procedures and findings here, and concentrate, rather, on summarizing some of the major conclusions that have emerged from the series of studies and considering some of the implications of these findings for a theory of perceptual development. Our procedure in most of these studies has been to present the subject with two simultaneous tape-recorded messages, one in a man's voice and one in a woman's voice, played over external speakers. The subject's task is to repeat the message spoken by one of the voices after the voices have stopped. The messages are brief ones, composed of simple English words which even our youngest subjects can easily articulate. We have worked primarily with children ranging in age between five and fourteen, although we have done some work with groups of elderly people. It is clear that, during middle childhood, there is great improvement in the ability to listen selectively. Not only are older children more accurate and complete in their reports of the desired voice, but they seldom report words spoken by the wrong voice. Younger children more often make intrusive errors — that is, they report the words spoken by the voice which they were asked to ignore.

One must ask whether the young child's difficulties with this task were perceptual, or whether they reflect a difficulty in producing the desired response. I shall now put this question in the form of a hypothesis (II-A) for analysis.

Hypothesis II-A. The increasing ability to select a wanted stimulus is an artifact of the increasing ability to report the wanted stimulus, rather than to perceive it.

As noted above, my colleagues and I attempt to use words and phrases which can easily be repeated by children as young as kindergarten age, but still it is possible that young children have more difficulty pronouncing them than older ones. In a recent study (Maccoby & Leifer, 1968), we asked our subjects to repeat what a single voice said, when the second voice was silent. We then asked them to select one voice when the second voice *was* present. We then used the difference between performances under these two conditions as the best reflection of the difficulty of selection per se. The difference score was much greater for younger children than older ones. This was true both for easy stimuli, on which all age groups performed almost perfectly with the single voice speaking alone, and the more difficult stimuli, where the younger children were slightly less accurate than older ones under the single-voice conditions. It should be noted that the response the child must produce is the same under the two conditions — the only difference is that in the one case he must shut out a distracting voice, and in the other case he need not do so. We conclude that

75

the greater difficulty the young child has in ignoring the unwanted voice lies at some point on the intake side of things, before the point of organizing the response is reached. On the basis of existing evidence concerning audition, Hypothesis II-A is disconfirmed. We do not know what role response factors play in visual selection tasks.

What, then, is the nature of the young child's difficulty in selective listening? We considered the possibility that it lay in peripheral masking. When two voices speak at one time, the sound signal arriving at the ear is a complex one in which certain elements in each voice mask certain elements in the other voice. Perhaps masking effects are greater for younger than older children, either because of a lower level of auditory acuity or because of defective interpretation of masked signals. This possibility is set forth in Hypothesis II-B.

Hypothesis II-B. The age increases in the ability to select a wanted auditory stimulus are a function of decreasing effects of peripheral masking.

We have controlled for peripheral masking in two ways. In one experiment, we contrasted dichotic listening with listening when the two voices came over separate external speakers (Maccoby & Konrad, 1966). With the external speakers, there is masking at the ear; with dichotic presentation, there is not. All age groups were able to select one voice more accurately than the other under the dichotic conditions, but the improvement was no greater for younger than older subjects. In another experiment (Maccoby & Leifer, 1968), masking was eliminated by having the two voices alternate. For example, the man's voice might say "this . . . is . . . good . . . grass" (leaving spaces between the words), and the woman's voice would say ". . . if . . . you . . . clean . . . up," so that the words of the two speakers did not actually coincide in time and there was no masking at the ear. The words arrived at the ears of the subject in the following order: "this if is you good clean grass up." The subject is asked to sort out the message on the basis of the sex of the speaker, and to report only one of the two messages. Younger children have considerably greater difficulty with this task than do older children.

Thus, even when peripheral masking is eliminated, young children continue to perform poorly on a selective listening task. They are no more helped than older children by the elimination of this masking. Therefore, Hypothesis II-B is disconfirmed, and we may next consider the role of preparatory set.

Hypothesis II-C. Young children cannot establish a selective set in advance of stimulation, and make use of it to focus attention on certain attributes of a complex stimulus input.

Among adults presented with visual displays, a prior set does help selective perception under certain experimental conditions. However, age changes in the utility of a set, or the conditions under which it improves performance, have not been traced with visual materials. For audition, my colleagues and I have used the experimental design described earlier (p. 75) in which performance with a prior set is compared with performance when the selection signal comes after stimulation. We have found that a prior signal improves the selective listening performance of subjects in all the age groups we have studied — children from five to fourteen and adults in their sixties, seventies, and early eighties. However, the preparatory signal improves performance to approximately the same degree at all the different ages studied. There are substantial changes with age in the accuracy of selective listening to two simultaneous voices. The performance improves during childhood and deteriorates in old age (see Maccoby, Jones, & Konrad, 1968), but these age changes are of the same order of magnitude when the listener has a prior set as they are when he has a post-stimulus signal. The availability of a prestimulus signal does not in any way account for the age changes. It may be of interest to note that we have used different time intervals over which a preparatory set must operate: we have compared a selection signal that occurs immediately before the stimulus with a no-prior-signal condition; and we have also compared a prior signal which is given once and then must be retained in memory over a series of trials with a condition in which the selection signal recurs throughout the series of trials. Neither of these experimental variations interacts with the age of the subject. Hypothesis II-C is disconfirmed.

It should be noted that although young children can make as much use of a preparatory signal to listen to only one voice as older children can, they nevertheless make more intrusive errors than older children, and this is true under both prior- and post-signal conditions. That is, they cannot so easily keep the two voices separate, even when they have successfully set themselves in advance for one of the voices.

In the studies in which we compared a prior selection signal with a post-stimulus signal, we found that the utility of such a signal did not depend on opportunities to orient the ears toward a source of sound (Maccoby & Konrad, 1967). Thus, in audition, there is clear evidence of selective processes that occur after the nature of the stimulation reaching the sense organs has been determined.

We know, then, that young children can establish a set to listen selectively to only a certain portion of a complex auditory stimulus — at least, they can do so if they are asked to select on the basis of a cue which is well discriminated. This finding may be considered from the standpoint of Broadbent's "filter" theory. Broadbent (1958) has described selective listening as a process of successive filtering in which the listener first identifies, or codes, the messages on the basis of some rather gross quality such as its color (if the stimuli are visual), or whether it is the right or left ear which is receiving the message, or the sex of the speaker's voice. On the basis of this first coding or filtering, the listener decides whether he wants to know more about the message or not; if not, he discards it; if he does, he identifies and codes more attributes of the stimulus. Recent work has indicated that the process is not quite like this — that selection of one channel is more like turning down the amplitude of the unwanted channel, rather than shutting it out altogether. In any case, the existing work does support the view that incoming information is processed in stages. For this kind of multistage processing to work, it would obviously be important for the listener to do the first-stage processing quickly and efficiently. Certain kinds of selective cues can be used more efficiently than others. For example, Triesman (1964) taped two messages in the same voice, and asked the subject to select one of them on the basis of the content of the message. This has proved to be a much more difficult task than selecting between messages spoken in different voices. Young children would surely have especially great difficulty selecting on the basis of content. They could not be expected, for example, to listen to a message on politics, while ignoring one on gardening, for they simply would not know enough about the content to distinguish between them. This suggests the developmental principle stated as Hypothesis II-D.

Hypothesis II-D. Although younger children are able to use selective cues as a basis for first-stage filtering, there are fewer cues which they can use for this purpose than is true for older children.

With increasing perceptual experience, which permits the child to discriminate between (or "code") more and more classes of stimuli, a larger range of cues becomes available for first-stage selection. There are certain stimulus attributes, such as color, motion, intensity, which can be discriminated by the newborn infant, and hence these may always be available as selective cues. Other discriminations must be learned.

Neisser (1967) has distinguished between "attentive" and "preattentive" processes. "Preattentive" processes, he argues, are global, serving merely to distinguish (segregate) figures or objects from one another, some of which may then be more fully analyzed through the processes of focal attention. He suggests that with increasing experience, there are more and more features of the stimulus complex which can be recognized "preattentively," without focal attention having to be directed to them. This would mean, for example, that we can come to recognize certain familiar objects out of the corner of the eye with a very brief glance and without taking in much detail, whereas on our first encounters with the object we should have had to study it and take note of a number of detailed features. Translating this point into the language used by Broadbent and Triesman, it would mean (as Hypothesis II-D states) that, with cognitive development, there are more and more portions of a complex stimulus input that can be handled with a first-stage filter. There is a difference, however. In filter theory, the sorting is done by attributes or dimensions; for Neisser, it is done by whole objects. It is a little difficult to see how the hypothesis concerning the holistic quality of preattentive processes applies to hearing, but Neisser believes that it does, with certain gross, easily discriminated features of simultaneous messages being used to segregate the messages from one another so that a selected message can be processed in detail through analysis by synthesis.

These considerations suggest that whatever makes stimuli maximally discriminable will assist the first-stage filtering process. It should be easier to select one of two voices if they are unlike rather than like. It should be easier to select all red stimuli and ignore all green ones than to select all red stimuli and ignore all bright pink ones. Beyond this, the familiarity of the stimuli should make a difference. There is a substantial amount of literature indicating that familiar stimuli are more easily discriminated from one another than are unfamiliar ones, other things being equal. This would mean, for example, that it should be easier to select one of two familiar voices than one of two unfamiliar voices. Older children, having had more opportunities to learn to discriminate cues, should be able to make use of more cues and finer distinctions for the purposes of first-stage filtering. However, the relevant comparative studies across age levels have not been done, so the hypothesis remains untested. In any case, using cues that they can already discriminate at a high level of accuracy (such as sex of voice), young children should be quite efficient at the first-stage filtering step.

However, the discriminability of stimuli should be important not only at the first stage of the selection process, but in the analysis and recognition of the selected set of stimuli during the second stage. That is, having selected a female voice, a subject must still recognize the words the woman's voice has spoken. If the unwanted voice has only been attenuated during the first-stage filtering process, not shut out altogether, it still constitutes a noisy background for the wanted material and as such should impede recognition. To determine what qualities cause a stimulus to be easily recognized under these noisy conditions, one must again consider the effects of variation in word familiarity. There is ample evidence that the speed of recognition of a stimulus — whether it is presented to the ear or to the eye — is greater for familiar stimuli than for unfamiliar ones. It is not entirely clear, however, whether this should mean that familiarity of the stimuli will facilitate selective listening. The problem is that both the material to be selected and the material to be ignored may vary in familiarity. If the material which the perceiver wishes to ignore is familiar, will it break through the "attentional barrier" and be recognized, thus interfering with the selection of the desired material?

In one experiment, Maccoby and Konrad (1967) varied the familiarity of both the material to be selected and the material to be shut out. In this experiment, familiar material was more easily selected. It was also true that the familiarity of the unwanted material affected performance, which would mean that the first-stage selection on the basis of the sex of the speaker's voice was imperfect. But it was not true that familiarity in the unwanted material was always detrimental to performance; rather, there was a contrast effect. The two voices were most easily separated — presumably, most easily discriminated — when their words were of different familiarity levels. Thus, high familiarity in the material to be shut out helped performance when it coincided with a low level of familiarity in the voice to be selected, but it hurt performance when it coincided with highly familiar words spoken by the target voice. Similarly, a low level of familiarity in the unwanted voice could either hurt or help performance, depending on the level of familiarity of the words spoken simultaneously by the target voice. Thus, at least in this particular selective task, familiarity operates somewhat differently than it does in simple perception; it operates as a dimension along which stimuli can differ, and (as with physical stimulus dimensions) the more different the wanted and unwanted messages are with respect to this dimension, the more easily can one of the competing messages be perceived.

It should be noted that, in the study just described, familiarity was not a dimension being used for selection — that is, the subjects were not being asked to listen only to familiar words and ignore unfamiliar ones. They were asked to listen to a man's voice and ignore a woman's voice, or vice versa, and the familiarity of the materials was simply an additional characteristic of the stimuli, unrelated to the selecting dimension. The selecting dimension is related to first-stage filtering, or preattentional processes, and I suggested in Hypothesis II-D that perceptual learning would increase the number of stimulus characteristics that would be used for sorting at this stage. Additional characteristics of the stimulus (characteristics other than those used for initial selection) presumably become relevant during the second stage — relevant to the recognition of stimulus materials once they have been selected through whatever sorting processes operate at the first stage. I am arguing that the subject's past perceptual experience is relevant here too, and that younger children will be at a disadvantage whenever they lack the experience or training that will permit them to discriminate those attributes of a stimulus that are most relevant to distinguishing it from the background and recognizing it. Perhaps the point is almost too obvious to be worth making, but for the sake of completeness I include it here as Hypothesis II-E.

Hypothesis II-E. The age improvement in selective perceiving is a function of discrimination learning, which determines how easily a stimulus can be identified in a noisy background.

Multiple Selective Sets

Up till now, I have been discussing the processes of selecting a single stimulus, or a set of stimuli sharing a certain characteristic, but I shall now consider multiple selective sets, or divided attention. As adults, we can pay attention to two things at one time — witness the busy executive who prides himself on being able to take two telephone calls at once, with a telephone propped on each shoulder. There has been much research on the division of attention, again almost none of it developmental. The work on vigilance and dichotic listening with adults seems to indicate that we do not attend to two messages at precisely the same moment; we switch attention from one "channel" to another fairly rapidly. During the moments when we are not attending to a particular message, we hold it briefly in some sort of short-term store.

Dividing attention must be a more complex process than selecting a single message. Attending to two messages involves everything that is involved in single attention, plus the additional processes of switching attention from one part of the total input to another and the additional burden upon memory and search processes that arises from attempting to recognize more material in a given period of time. The simplest hypothesis concerning the development of the ability to divide attention is that in Hypothesis III.

HYPOTHESIS III

Hypothesis III. Selecting simultaneously two or more portions of a complex stimulus is more difficult than selecting a single portion, and is a skill which develops more slowly during childhood.

In the experiment described above (Maccoby & Leifer, 1968) in which the subjects were presented with two alternating voices, the subjects were asked to attend to only one voice and to ignore the other. In a second condition of the same experiment, the subjects were asked to attend to both voices, reporting one voice and then the other. The voice to be reported first was specified. Figure 1 shows the results. At all the ages studied, children performed better when selecting one voice than when listening to

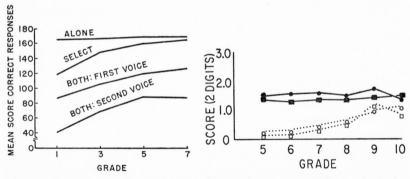

Figure 1. Mean score of correct responses (maximum score 171) on alternating voices task by Ss in grades 1, 3, 5, and 7. *Figure 2.* Mean recall for two digits per ear in dichotic listening when order and laterality are both taken into account. Solid circles and squares stand for first presentation; open for second. Circles designate results for the right ear; squares, the left. Reproduced from Inglis & Sykes, *Journal of Experimental Child Psychology*, 1967, 5, 480–488, by permission of Academic Press, Inc.

both. It is especially interesting that they performed so poorly with the *first* voice reported under the "both voices" condition. Here they are reporting precisely the same words as those called for under the select condition, and in both conditions they are reporting immediately after stimulation. But the instruction to attend to both, and presumably the process of holding the second voice in memory while reporting the first, interferes with performances on the first voice. Figure 1 also shows that skill in the divided attention task develops more slowly than skill in simple selection. The superiority of performance in the "select" condition over that with the first voice in the "both voices" condition is greater for the older subjects. The age interaction is significant at $<.001$ level. Thus, Hypothesis III is confirmed.

The evidence for Hypothesis III is not altogether positive, however. In two other studies (Hagen, 1967; Maccoby & Hagen, 1965), children were presented with a visual task. Under one experimental condition, they were not asked to divide attention, whereas under another condition, they had to remain vigilant for an auditory signal while continuing to respond to the visual displays. Under the divided-attention condition, performance on the central visual task was reduced at all age levels, but the rate of improvement with age was no greater for the undivided-attention conditions than for the divided-attention condition. There is support of Hypothesis III, then, for a selective listening task, but not for a task in which the subjects must process information in two modalities.

Returning to the discussion of the selective listening study in which subjects were asked to report both voices, we see (Fig. 1) that performance on the second voice reported is poorer at all age levels than performance on the first; the shape of the two age curves is very similar. These findings may be compared with those of Inglis and Sykes (1967). They presented two different sets of digits simultaneously, one set to each ear with both sets being spoken by the same man's voice. Figure 2 shows their results for two-digit sets. For children aged five through ten, there was no change with age in the accuracy of reporting the first set. However, for the second set, there was considerable age improvement. Their results for three-digit sets showed similar age trends. Inglis and Sykes's age trends, then, are similar to those reported in Figure 1 for the second-reported voice. But for the first-reported voice, we found an increase with age in the accuracy of report, whereas Inglis and Sykes did not. In fact, the magnitude of the age changes in our data was approximately the same for the first and second voice (see Fig. 1). The difference between the two sets of data is probably not a function of memory load. In our studies, stimuli were varied with respect to the length and sequentiality of the phrases spoken by the two voices. We obtained substantial age improvement with the first-reported voice for both three-word sequential strings and three-word nonsequential strings — the latter being similar in informational load to the three-digit sets of digits used by Inglis and Sykes. Three digits, or three non-numerical words, are within the memory span of children of all the ages studied. It is therefore likely that the age improvement on the first voice in our study reflects an increasing ability to keep the two messages separated on the basis of the sex of the speaker's voice, rather than an increase in memory capacity. But with respect to the second-reported voice, memory capacity is more probably involved. Inglis and Sykes believe that this is so; referring to Broadbent's theory of the way in which information is processed in dichotic listening, they say (1967, pp. 480–481):

The perceptual system can only pass information successively, whereas the storage system can hold any excess information which may arrive when the perceptual system is already fully occupied in dealing with information from another channel. In DLP (dichotic listening performance) the digits reproduced first in sequence have, by this hypothesis, been processed directly through the first of these systems, whereas the material recalled second in sequence has spent some time in storage. Material held in store is subject to trace decay, which explains why more errors of recall appear in the material reproduced second in sequence.

In interpreting their own findings, they say further: "Short-term storage capacity would appear, as expected, to increase with age in childhood." Inglis and Sykes do not specify precisely what is implied in the term "increasing short-term storage capacity." They refer to the short-term storage system (where the message of the second voice must be held during the report of the first) as one which is subject to "trace decay," a decay which presumably occurs fairly rapidly with the passage of time. Taking this suggestion literally, we can formulate Hypothesis III-A, concerning age changes in performance on tasks which call for divided attention.

Hypothesis III-A. In divided-attention tasks, younger children perform less well on the second-reported portion of the stimulus because their memory traces fade faster.

The first problem in analyzing this hypothesis has to do with the meaning we shall give to the term *memory trace.* Does it mean a brief after-image that maintains the stimulus very much in its original form? Atkinson and Shiffrin (1967) distinguish this kind of stimulus trace, which they consider to be part of the "sensory register" from the "short-term store," to which information is transferred from the sensory register, and where the stored material decays more slowly — over a period of perhaps thirty seconds. A certain amount of coding or other processing of the input occurs at the time of transfer to the short-term store. The distinction between sensory register and short-term store has proved useful to researchers in vision because there is evidence that the visual input is often translated into auditory-verbal form as it goes into the short-term store. For audition, the distinction is not so clear. Neisser, in his discussion of the duration of the "echoic" memory trace, seems to be referring to a single trace process, not two occurring in rapid succession. Is it really a likely possibility that the traces in the sensory register or those in the short-term store fade more rapidly in young children than they do in older children and adults? I noted earlier that, although Sperling did chart the time function for the decay of the post-stimulus trace for vision in adults, no one has studied developmental changes in the rate of fading of this trace. There is the literature on eidetic imagery, in which individuals have been identified for whom a vivid post-stimulus visual image appears to last much longer than it does for most adult perceivers. It was originally alleged that eidetic imagery declined with age and was fairly common in children (Jaensch, 1930). Haber and Haber (1964) in recent work have verified the fact that eidetic children do exist, but found that they were fairly rare and that it was difficult to trace age changes in the incidence of the phenomenon because of the difficulty of obtaining adequate reports from children under six or seven. Doob (1964; 1965) in cross-cultural studies of two nonliterate cultural groups in Africa, reports that eidetic imagery is considerably more common among such groups than in Western societies, that it is more common among rural than urban African people, and that among urban Africans, it is more common among children than adults. In the United States, it has been found that eidetic imagery is more common among retarded than among normal children (Siipola & Hayden, 1965). All these findings suggest that a long-lasting stimulus trace is a primitive phenomenon, one which declines during the normal process of growth and the onset of literacy as more conceptual modes of information storage come into play. Heinz Werner took this view of eidetic imagery (Werner, 1948), and it is consistent with Bruner's discussion of the developmental shift from "iconic" to "symbolic" representation (Bruner, 1964).

As noted above, the post-stimulus visual image need not be the same thing as the short-term store where some representation of the visual input can be briefly stored. It is possible that the visual image does not fade so quickly in young children, but that the representation in short-term store fades more rapidly than would be true for adults. Much more detailed information is needed concerning the temporal decay functions in children of different ages, for both auditory and visual inputs. Hypothesis III-A remains an open possibility, but it seems to me an unlikely one.

As for the problem of young children's poor performance on the second voice in the divided-attention task, it does seem likely that this poor performance must have something to do with deficient memory function. However, the deficit may be of a different kind than the simple fading of a trace with time, as suggested in Hypothesis III-B.

Hypothesis III-B. In divided attention tasks, the act of reporting the first message interferes more with the retention of the second one for younger than older children.

In working with elderly subjects, my colleagues and I have found that when the subjects were asked to report both voices, they performed especially poorly on the second voice. During this task, the elderly subjects often said that they had clearly heard both voices, but that the very process of reporting the first voice seemed to wipe out the memory of the second one. An experiment on this issue has been conducted by Tom Jones (unpublished, summarized in Maccoby, in press) using middle-aged and elderly subjects on a divided-attention task. Jones found that response-interference is a much greater factor than simple fading of the memory trace in lowering performance on the second-reported message. If this is true for elderly subjects, it may be true for children as well, although the relevant experiments tracing age changes in response interference have not been done. Hypothesis III-B remains as an untested possibility. It is worth noting, however, that in Jones's experiment, where the elderly subjects performed very poorly on the divided-attention task, response interference was no greater a factor in their performance than in that of the middle-aged subjects. It may turn out that in studies with children, response interference, although important in determining the level of performance, is no more important for one age group than another. The outcome might depend on the degree to which different age groups use unfilled time for rehearsal. Response interference probably occurs because it prevents rehearsal. If younger children rehearse more, or *need* rehearsal more to keep a trace alive, then an interpolated response will hurt their performance more.

Hypothesis III-C. Young children are not so efficient as older ones in "coding" or "chunking" the material being held in short-term store, and so cannot hold as much.

Thinking in these terms implies that the relevant short-term storage process is not the post-stimulus image, where the input would appear in raw or unprocessed form, but in a subsequent short-term store of the sort defined and described by Atkinson and Shiffrin (1967). In a divided-attention task, if the message to be reported second is entered into such a store while the first message is being reported, then the more "codable" it is, the more efficiently should it be held for the subsequent report.

As a test of this hypothesis, I can compare our subjects' performance on sequentially probable phrases versus sequentially improbable phrases. The stimulus materials used in our divided-attention task (Maccoby & Leifer, 1968) included both kinds of phrases. For example, in one item the male voice said "did go up," while the female voice said "are just right." In another item, the two voices said, respectively: "good for went" and "near to soon." There were also four-word phrases, some sequential, some non-sequential. From Hypothesis III-C one can predict that younger children will not take as much advantage of the "chunking" possibilities of the sequential phrases while they hold the second-voice message in store. Consequently, the sequentiality of the phrases will not make much difference in their performance on the second voice. For older children, the more sequential phrases should be more easily reported for the second voice. A further prediction, this time from Inglis and Sykes's formulation, is that the "chunkability" of the materials will not make much difference for the reports of the first voice at any age level, since these reports are coming directly from the "perceptual system" rather than the short-term store.

The first prediction is sustained. Sequentiality of the stimuli improves second-voice performance more for older than younger children (the age interaction has an F value of 8.41, df $= 3$, $p < .01$). The second is only partly sustained. Sequentiality is *not* of greater value for older than younger children on reports of the first voice (F for the age interaction is 1.48,

87

n.s.). This is in accord with the prediction that sequentiality should interact with age only for the second voice, not the first. However, sequentiality does make a first-order difference; that is, for the first voice, sequential phrases are reported more accurately than non-sequential ones at all age levels. Do sequential verbal stimuli have some additional advantage in selective listening, other than in being more chunkable for short-term storage? This question must be left open, but meanwhile there is some evidence in support of Hypothesis III-C.

To summarize briefly the main points uncovered so far: There is evidence of improvement during childhood in the orientation of the sense organs toward the most informative portions of a stimulus complex. Beyond this, there is improvement in post-stimulation selective processes, and in the ability to divide attention so as to select more than one of several simultaneously available messages. I have discussed a number of hypotheses concerning the nature of the young child's deficit, and many of these explorations have yielded negative results. We know more about what the problem is not than about what it is. Although the relevant evidence has not been explicitly drawn together above, it seems to me that it is not especially useful to think of the deficit in terms of the child's having a more limited "information processing capacity" or "memory storage capacity" in the usual meaning of these terms. Rather, the problem would seem to be that the "capacity" the young child has is not efficiently employed. Some of the evidence has pointed to the probable importance of discrimination learning and coding or "chunking" processes, although the evidence is sparse. But the discrimination problem is of a special kind, for stimuli which the child has learned enough about so that he can readily identify them when they are presented alone become unidentifiable when they are part of a more complex multiple input. It is the effect of the unwanted material on the perception of the wanted material that is the heart of the problem. Wohlwill (1962) states the developmental principle succinctly: "the amount of irrelevant information that can be tolerated without affecting the response increases" (with age).

Why should this be so? There are several different ways in which the introduction of irrelevant material affects the response. In some instances, the young child simply responds to the irrelevant portions of a stimulus input, as in the instances when he reports the wrong voice in a selective listening experiment (an intrusive error). Sometimes he fails to respond at all; sometimes, he fails to segregate the two stimuli from one another and gives a combined or merged response. An example of this kind of thing may be seen in the response given when one voice says *center* and the other says *whistle*. A child may report that he heard *sister*, or even *whister*. Older children are less likely than younger to make merged responses that are nonsense words (see Maccoby & Konrad, 1967). The child's difficulty in "disembedding" the wanted stimulus from its context has a familiar parallel in visual perception. As Witkin reported many years ago (1950), there is a substantial age improvement in performance on the Gottschaldt figures, a task in which the subject must locate a simple figure embedded in a complex one. The nature of the young child's difficulty has been conceptualized in a number of ways. Heinz Werner (1948) described the young child's perceptions as global or undifferentiated. In his famous example of a four-year-old child looking at a drawing of a duck on a rock, Werner suggests that the child sees the entire picture, rock and all, as *duck*. Werner describes the child's perception in this instance as "diffusely organized" and "homogeneous." In cases of this kind, it is difficult to know whether the "diffuseness" has occurred in the perception or in the labeling of what is perceived. It is entirely possible that the child has seen the line that separates the duck from the rock, or that he has seen one closed figure constituting a subpart of a larger closed figure (duck-on-rock). It may simply be the case that he has learned to use the verbal label *duck* for the more inclusive rather than the less inclusive pattern. One could surely find examples in which the child errs in the opposite direction — when, for example, he sees a picture of a front door and calls it *house*. Werner holds, however, that the child's perceptions are holistic — that there is greater influence of the "totality of the organization" on his percept. He cites as evidence the experiment by Heiss and Sander (reported in Heiss, 1930), in which children were asked to find a missing block. Younger children had more difficulty locating the block when it was embedded in a design than when it was part of an unorganized jumble of blocks. For older children, the embeddedness made little difference. Werner's position has much in common with that of Piaget, who also emphasizes the greater importance of the Gestalt "field" properties in the perceptions of young children, and holds that the child's earliest schemas (to which he presumably matches inputs in recognition) are topological representations and, in the beginning, very simple ones.

HYPOTHESIS IV

The implications of this position for selective perception would appear to be as follows: If we ask a child to select a portion of a stimulus complex, his success will depend upon whether the larger context forms a "good Gestalt" — and whether it forms a better one than the subportion to be selected. If it does, the child would not be able to differentiate the desired portion from its context; indeed, the theory in its strongest form would imply that under these conditions, the child would not perceive the subparts at all, but only the larger organized whole. If the subpart to be selected has strong organizational properties of its own, on the other hand, the child would perceive the part and not the whole. This hypothesis was tested by Elkind, Keogler, and Go (1964). They worked with children aged four through nine, and presented them with drawings in which objects were made up of highly recognizable subparts. For example, a scooter was formed out of candy canes, and an airplane had a potato for a body and carrots for wings. The experimenters deliberately biased the drawings so that the organization of the parts was stronger than that of the wholes. The subjects were asked to describe what they saw. The younger children saw primarily the subparts and failed to perceive the larger whole which they composed. The older children more often saw both the parts and the whole. Elkind et al. cite earlier research with stimuli which were similarly designed but for which the wholes were more familiar and more strongly organized than the parts. With such stimuli, younger children more often saw the whole only, and older children saw both the wholes and the parts. Elkind et al. argue from these results that development is not characterized by a change from perception of a whole to a more differentiated perception of parts, but that younger children tend to focus on whatever level of the stimulus is the most strongly organized. They say further (1964, p. 87):

Centering, as it is used by Piaget, implies not only a domination by field effects, but also a kind of fixation on the dominant figure and an inability spontaneously to shift perspective so as to perceive the configuration in a new way . . . In part-whole perception, decentering involves a shift of focus from whole to part or vice versa. Our finding that there is a general increase with age in the ability of children to perceive both part and whole is therefore in accord with the decentering position.

This position leads to a hypothesis concerning selective perception.

Hypothesis IV. Younger children's selective perceptions will be more handicapped than those of older children if the material to be selected is part of a larger stronger configuration, or if it contains strongly organized subparts.

Configurations whose boundaries do not coincide with the material to be selected may lead the young child to take in too much or too little.

Hypothesis IV appears to have a good probability of being true. Still, it does not account for many of the phenomena of selective perception reviewed above. When two voices speak simultaneously, there is no reason to believe that a combination word (made up of components of the two stimulus words) has any stronger a "configuration" — whatever that may mean in audition! — than the original words, or that the whole word that intrudes from the non-target voice has stronger configurational properties. Yet these intrusions occur, and more frequently for younger subjects. We must still deal with the fact that, configurational properties aside, younger children cannot so easily shut out unwanted material.

It may be possible to gain some insight into the complex interactions among discrimination, selection, and the division of attention by examining some of the recent findings on incidental learning. In a study done several years ago, John Hagen and I reasoned that if the young child's perceptions were not as selective as those of the older person's, then the young child ought to notice more of the task-irrelevant components of a display, and do more incidental learning. In one study, we found that the amount of incidental learning in a visual task remained constant from grades one through five, and then declined significantly at the seventh grade level (Maccoby & Hagen, 1965). In that study, however, the central task required the child to notice the portion of a stimulus which would ordinarily be the background, and the incidental part of the task asked for memory of what would ordinarily be the figure. The results, therefore, might simply have been an example of Hypothesis IV above — that younger children are more bound by the configurational properties of the stimulus. Hagen did a second experiment (Hagen, 1967) in which the configurational properties of the central and incidental components were equated. Again he found no significant age change in incidental learning from grades one through five, and a drop-off at the seventh grade (under distraction conditions). Crane and Ross (1967) found that when an initially irrelevant cue was made redundant during over-training trials in a discrimination task, and then later made the relevant positive cue, there was positive transfer for second-graders but not for sixth-graders. These findings suggest that the younger subjects were attending more to the irrelevant, redundant cue. Since only two age levels were studied, we do not know precisely the point at which the change occurred, but the results are consistent with the Maccoby and Hagen studies (and with the selective listening work) in indicating a greater tendency for the entire group of older children to ignore task-irrelevant material. If this were the only developmental process at work, however, it is strange that the decline appeared only at this age. We have evidence from many of the studies reported above that an age improvement in selective processes occurs much earlier. A further problem in interpreting the findings is that there is evidence from an early study by Stevenson (1954) that incidental learning *increases* with age during the preschool years. Two recent studies (Hale, Miller, & Stevenson, 1968; Siegel & Stevenson, 1966) have shown that the relationship between age and incidental learning is indeed curvilinear. In both these studies, incidental learning increased through the age range from seven or eight through approximately twelve, and decreased at age thirteen or fourteen — again at approximately the seventh-grade level. We see, then, that up to early adolescence, there is an increase in the ability to report task-irrelevant information, and this occurs during a period when there is a substantial increase in the ability to shut out such information!

Evidently, there is a difference between having one's performance impaired by the presence of irrelevant information, and being able to report what that information is. It was noted above that, in the selective listening tasks, younger children made more intrusive errors. In these instances, they did actually report the irrelevant information. In more instances, however, the presence of the irrelevant information simply led to an inability to respond at all. The subject reported that he could not distinguish what was said, and this was true even in the studies where peripheral masking was eliminated. In the cases where the introduction of irrelevant material led to the inability to report anything, it is likely that the child did not discriminate the components of the complex stimulus from one another.

For incidental learning to occur, the subject must discriminate and identify the irrelevant material, and store it separately. This means that such learning involves, to some degree, the division of attention — the simultaneous processing of more than one message at a time. We have seen that such dual processing is more difficult than single selection, and that skill in divided-attention tasks probably increases more slowly with age than for simple selection. It is not surprising, then, that incidental learning should increase during early childhood. Why should it drop off at age twelve or thirteen? By this age, it would seem that the individual has developed his selective skills to the point where he can quickly discriminate only those attributes of the stimulus that permit him to decide whether it is wanted or unwanted. He does not need to identify its other attributes if the stimulus is unwanted, but if he does not do so, the unwanted material will not be stored in retrievable form and will not be available in an incidental learning test. As we have seen, young children can do this preattentive or first-stage selection fairly easily when the basis for selection is a physical quality of the stimulus such as color or quality of voice. However, in the incidental learning studies reported above the irrelevant material was usually just a different symbol or outline drawing (or in one case — Hagen — a different *class* of drawings) than the relevant material. I suggest that the child under twelve or thirteen has difficulty handling such distinctions preattentively and hence attends focally to both sets of material, with the result that incidental learning occurs.

I have returned to the distinction between "preattentive" processes, or first-stage filtering, and focal attention. Can these terms be defined more precisely? Neisser (1967), in a reformulation of the motor theory of speech, argues that to attend focally to one conversation in preference to others is "to synthesize a series of linguistic units which match it successfully" (p. 213). He takes a similar view with respect to visual search and recognition, suggesting that focal attention involves "analysis by synthesis," a process in which the perceiver generates an attempted match for the incoming material and compares this synthesis with the stored records of previous syntheses. It is obvious that this theory has many implications for developmental psychology. What kind of "match" is a young child capable of generating? If understanding someone else's speech involves synthesizing a matching series of linguistic units, why is the child able to understand complex forms of speech before he can produce them overtly? These questions are beyond the scope of this paper. For the present it is sufficient to say that Neisser's distinction between preattentive and attentive processes has proved useful in understanding existing research on stimulus selection and its development through childhood.

A final point: Throughout this paper, the discussion has focused upon the selective processes of which children are capable when they are instructed to select a given portion of the stimulus complex. In structuring the problem this way, there is danger of overlooking what may be the most important developmental change of all: the change in the degree to which perceptions *are* selective in the normal course of events, without explicit instructions to the perceiver. It is true, of course, that infants are selective; they tend to attend more to stimuli which are novel or salient in some other way. However, it is reasonable to say that an infant is usually looking *at* a stimulus rather than looking *for* something in the stimulus pattern. Thus, I close with a final hypothesis, V, concerning development.

Hypothesis V. With increasing age, the child's perceptions are more and more dominated by organized search patterns that are related to sustained "plans" or ongoing behavior patterns of the perceiver.

References

Atkinson, R. C., & R. M. Shiffrin. Human memory: A proposed system and its control processes. Technical Report No. 110, Institute for Mathematical Studies in the Social Sciences, Stanford University, March 1967.

Broadbent, D. E. *Perception and communication.* New York: Pergamon Press, 1958.

Bruner, J. The course of cognitive growth. *American Psychologist,* 1964, 19, 1–15.

Crane, N. L., & L. E. Ross. A developmental study of attention to cue redundancy. *Journal of Experimental Child Psychology,* 1967, 5, 1–15.

Doob, L. W. Eidetic images among the Ibo. *Ethnology,* 1964, 3, 357–362.

———. Exploring eidetic imagery among the Kamba of Central Kenya. *Journal of Social Psychology,* 1965, 67, 3–22.

Elkind, D., R. R. Keogler, & E. Go. Studies in perceptual development, II. Part-whole perception. *Child Development,* 1964, 35, 81–90.

Fantz, R. L. The origin of form perception. *Scientific American,* 1961, 204, 66–72.

Gibson, E. J. Perceptual development, in H. W. Stevenson, ed., *Child psychology,* Yearbook of the National Society for the Study of Education, pp. 144–195. Chicago: University of Chicago Press, 1963.

Haber, R. N., & R. B. Haber. Eidetic imagery: I. Frequency. *Perceptual and Motor Skills,* 1964, 19, 131–138.

Hagen, J. W. The effect of distraction on selective attention. *Child Development,* 1967, 38, 685–694.

Hale, G. A., L. K. Miller, & H. W. Stevenson. Incidental learning of film content: A developmental study. *Child Development,* 1968, 39, 69–78.

Harris, C. S., & R. N. Haber. Selective attention and coding in visual perception. *Journal of Experimental Psychology,* 1963, 65, 328–333.

Heiss, A. Zum problem der isolierenden abstraktion. *Psychologische Studien,* 1930, 4, 285–318.

Inglis, J., & D. H. Sykes. Some sources of variation in dichotic listening performance in children. *Journal of Experimental Child Psychology,* 1967, 5, 480–488.

Jaensch, E. R. *Eidetic imagery and topological methods of investigation.* New York: Harcourt, 1930.

Lawrence, D. H., & D. L. LaBerge. Relationship between recognition accuracy and order of reporting stimulus dimensions. *Journal of Experimental Psychology,* 1956, 51, 12–18.

Maccoby, E. E. Selective auditory attention in children, in L. P. Lippsitt & C. C. Spiker, eds., *Advances in child development and behavior*, Vol. III, pp. 99–124. New York: Academic Press, 1967.

———. Age changes in the selective perception of verbal materials, in P. M. Kjeldergaard, ed., *The perception of language*. In press.

———, & J. Hagen. Effects of distraction upon central versus incidental recall: Developmental trends. *Journal of Experimental Child Psychology*, 1965, 2, 280–289.

Maccoby, E. E., T. M. Jones, & K. W. Konrad. Selective listening in later life, in S. S. Chown & K. F. Riegel, eds., *Psychological functioning in the normal aging and senile aged, Interdisciplinary Topics in Gerontology*, Vol. I, pp. 48–67. Basel & New York: S. Karger, 1968.

Maccoby, E. E., & K. W. Konrad. Age trends in selective listening. *Journal of Experimental Child Psychology*, 1966, 3, 113–122.

———. The effect of preparatory set on selective listening: Developmental trends. *Monographs of the Society for Research in Child Development*, 1967 (4, Serial No. 112).

Maccoby, E. E., & A. D. Leifer. Children's selective listening to alternating voices. Unpublished M.S., Laboratory of Human Development, Stanford University, 1968.

Mackworth, N. H., & J. S. Bruner. Selecting visual information during recognition by adults and children. Unpublished MS., Center for Cognitive Studies, Harvard University, 1966.

Neisser, U. R. *Cognitive psychology*. New York: Appleton, 1967.

Palestini, M., A. Davidovich, & R. Hernandez-Peon. The functional significance of centrifugal influences upon the retina. *Acta Neurologica Latinomer*, 1959, 5, 113–131.

Quay, H. C., R. L. Sprague, J. S. Werry, & M. M. McQueen. Conditioning visual orientation of conduct problem children in the classroom. *Journal of Experimental Child Psychology*, 1967, 5, 512–517.

Salapatek, P., & W. Kessen. Visual scanning of triangles by the human newborn. *Journal of Experimental Child Psychology*, 1966, 3, 155–167.

Siegel, A. W., & H. W. Stevenson. Incidental learning: A developmental study. *Child Development*, 1966, 37, 811–818.

Siipola, E. N., & S. D. Hayden. Exploring eidetic imagery among the retarded. *Perceptual and Motor Skills*, 1965, 21, 275–286.

Solley, C. M., & G. Murphy. *Development of the perceptual world*. New York: Basic Books, 1960.

Sperling, G. The information available in brief visual presentations. *Psychological Monographs*, 1960, 74 (11, Whole No. 498).

Stevenson, H. W. Latent learning in children. *Journal of Experimental Psychology*, 1954, 47, 17–21.

Sutton, S., P. Tueting, J. Zubin, & E. R. John. Information delivery and the sensory evoked potential. *Science*, 1967, 155, 1436–1439.

Treisman, A. M. Verbal cues, language, and meaning in selective attention. *American Journal of Psychology*, 1964, 77, 206–219.

Vurpillot, E. The development of scanning strategies and their relation to visual differentiation. *Journal of Experimental Child Psychology*, 1968, 6, 632–650.

Werner, H. *The comparative psychology of mental development*. Chicago: Follett, 1948; New York: Science Editions, 1961.

Witryol, S. L., L. M. Lowden, & J. F. Fagen. Incentive effects upon attention in children's discrimination learning. *Journal of Experimental Child Psychology*, 1967, 5, 94–108.

Wohlwill, J. F. From perception to inference: A dimension of cognitive development, in W. Kessen & C. Kuhlman, eds., Thought in the young child. *Monographs of the Society for Research in Child Development*, 1962, 27 (2, Serial No. 83), 87–107.

Zaporozhets, A. V. The development of perception in the preschool child, in P. Mussen, ed., European research in cognitive development. *Monographs of the Society for Research in Child Development*, 1965, 30 (2, Serial No. 100), 82–101.

Adolescent Attitudes and Behavior in Their Reference Groups within Differing Sociocultural Settings

IN SOCIAL psychology, the focal problem is the relation between the individual and his sociocultural setting. In this paper, we shall focus on our continuing research program initiated over ten years ago, which was conceived as basic research on the individual-group relationship during adolescence. The principal objectives of the program are theoretical and methodological.

It is our firm conviction that if basic research is to bear on the actualities of social behavior, and hence have valid applications, it must come to grips with at least these two major problems of theory and method: first, the interdisciplinary nature of the problem of the individual-group relationship, and second, the resulting necessity for attacking the problem with a combination of research methods, including both experimental and field methods, integrated in such a way that precise and valid accounts of the phenomena in question can be given.

In psychology, the unit of study is the individual; the data are his behavior during interactions that occur within an ecological and a cultural setting. These interactions and settings are the stimulus situations. Their complexity dictates that psychological data cannot be discrete bits of be-

NOTE: The research program reported in this paper was directed by Muzafer Sherif with support from the National Science Foundation, the Rockefeller Foundation, and in its initial stages, the Hogg Foundation for Mental Health. Carolyn W. Sherif collaborated in the research from its inception and had the primary responsibility in preparation of this paper.

havior lifted from their context. On the contrary, we have to study behavioral events *over time, in sequence,* noting their consequences in shaping the individual's attitudes and actions toward others, and toward significant activities and objects.

A basic assumption in our research has been that human social behavior, whether directed toward socially desirable or undesirable ends, can be accounted for more adequately within a context of interpersonal relationships. Characteristically, these interpersonal relationships occur within the bounds of groups — the family, age-mate groups, school and community groups — whose acceptance or rejection, approval or disapproval, and attribution of status and prestige are of serious personal concern. This means that, in addition to analysis of behavior at the psychological level, analysis at the sociological level is needed to conceptualize the stimulus side of the individual-group relationship. We have to place the attitude and behavior of the individual within the organization and the set of values or norms that count for him.

But this is not all. Small groups and interpersonal relations within them are not closed systems. Their organization, norms, and members' activities are affected by relevant features of the settings in which they interact — the nature and spatial arrangements of housing and recreational facilities, the standard of living, the cultural and educational level of the populace, and the prevailing reference scales defining what is undesirable and what is desirable in many respects. Finally, these specific settings are part of a larger society which conveys values and goals to its members, especially through the mass media and the educational system.

What is needed is research that specifies the ecological and sociocultural settings as they actually confront the individual, that locates him within the set of interpersonal relationships which count for him, that determines the values prevailing among people around him, and that relates his behavior over time to this context. Through the interrelation of findings at these various levels of analysis, the prediction of individual behavior may begin to appear feasible. The huge task of completing such research necessarily requires that we employ a combination of research methods and techniques — not merely side by side in insulated compartments, but in a coordinated way. Then, and only then, can we truly integrate the findings from experimental research, on the one hand, and field research, on the other.

During the course of our experiments on group formation and intergroup relations (Sherif, 1966; Sherif, Harvey, White, Hood, & Sherif, 1961; Sherif & Sherif, 1953), we developed procedures for the observation and measurement of interaction processes. Research on natural groups of adolescents extended and greatly refined the observational procedures (Sherif & Sherif, 1964). Both the group experiments and a series of laboratory studies permitted the development of methods to secure short-cut behavioral indicators of interpersonal attitudes, status and role expectations, and intergroup attitudes through cognitive functioning—namely, judgment and perception (see Sherif, 1967). Thus, our methodology was derived partly from experimentation and partly from field research in the course of the program itself.

The focus of the research program is on natural groups of adolescents as they interact in their natural surroundings, unaware that they are subjects of research interest. In this report, we shall first consider the properties of natural groups, derived both from a survey of the research literature and our own research. Next, we consider why such groups form so frequently among adolescents in modern societies and why they are so important in psychological development, especially in the re-formation of the self system during that transitional period of growth. With this background, we shall turn to findings from our research program, first summarizing illustrative generalizations about the relations between the sociocultural setting and individual attitudes; second, indicating our methods of research with emphasis on the study of interpersonal relationships and conformity-deviation relative to group norms; and finally, citing several experiments to illustrate the coordinated use of field and laboratory methods in the effort to attain valid generalizations.

The Research Program on Natural Groups of Adolescents

What are natural groups? Why is their study important? Among other things, natural groups are *not* casual encounters with people; they are not classroom groups in a school; they are not ad hoc collections of N persons of the kind studied in the great bulk of laboratory studies of "small groups." Nor is a natural group something that drops out of the blue in one piece, or that forms by spontaneous generation. *Natural group* is a convenient term from the point of view of the initial formation of the human group. A natural group is a human formation, consisting of a specifiable number of members, formed over a time span, through voluntary and informal interaction of individuals. In time, a natural group may or may not be codified as a recognized and formal organization. Thus, the natural group is not an esoteric phenomenon. The formation of a natural group seems to be a universal human process in various spheres of social life.

The minimum essential properties of any group consist of (a) a pattern or organization of roles and statuses and (b) a set of values or norms, at least in spheres of activity frequently engaged in by the group. One can say that the groupness of the group is directly proportional to the degree that the set of norms is shared by the members as their own felt values and that their interpersonal relationships are stabilized in reciprocal modes of behavior and mutual expectations. In natural groups, the pattern of statuses — that is, the relations between leader and follower — is not imposed from outside or through formal organization. Hence, as a general rule, leadership authority is not perceived as an autocratic imposition from outside. In our studies, we have records of such statements as "We have no leader," "We have no boss," and "We are all equal." Despite such expressions, members could be and were reliably ranked as first, second, third, and so on in terms of the frequency of their *effective initiative* in starting and in carrying on activities.

In brief, the natural group is a *reference group* for the individual member. It is a group whose acceptance the individual actively seeks, a group in which he aspires to amount to something, a group against whose yardsticks he gauges his own success or failure in relevant dimensions. The self picture of the individual is shaped, in no small part, by his reference group ties and by the yardsticks provided by his reference group.

Obviously, groups do not rise and function in a vacuum. The members' claims for attainment as well as the goals they are pursuing are relative to the setting of which they and their group are a part. That part of the setting that raises issues or problems for them in their moves toward goals is the sociocultural setting.

If an individual's attitudes and behavior are affected by his reference groups, and these groups, in turn, are related to the sociocultural setting of which they are parts, what does this imply for the study of human behavior? It means that, if we are seriously interested in the etiology of attitude and behavior, we have to study them amid influences ranging all the way from the society and the particular sociocultural setting of which he is a part down to the groups in which he actually moves and his own psychological make-up. Probably most psychologists would agree in principle that behavior is determined by such a gamut of influences. However, our research traditions and specializations do not encourage us to include the gamut of influences in our research designs. Instead, we are likely to end up studying groups or personality variables, or surveying attitudes, or studying cultural influences in isolation — paying only lip service to the fact that they act, react, and interact, shaping behavior in an interrelated way.

In designing our research on natural reference groups, we took literally the need to include at least the essentials from the entire gamut of influences, and we therefore organized the research into three interrelated parts. First, low, middle, and high socioeconomic areas with differing ethnic composition were chosen for study so that we could specify differences and reach generalizations common to all levels. Second, we obtained data on acceptable and objectionable behaviors and goals among individuals, groups, and areas, both to compare an individual's attitudes with those in his group and with those prevailing in its sociocultural setting and to compare attitudes in various areas. Third, groups of four to twelve teen-age boys (13–19 years), selected on the basis of their frequent and recurrent association, were studied intensively for six to twelve months by means of such techniques as observation, behavior ratings by regular observers and independent observers, informal sociometric tests, and situational tests. The distinctive strategy of our research is that the subjects are not aware that they are being observed.

It would be perfectly understandable to ask, Why go to the trouble of dealing with such a variety of different kinds of data, especially when a lot of them are not psychological data? The answer is that all this is necessary if we are ever to achieve theoretical formulations and analyses that are *valid*. It is precisely because we in psychology have been so buried in fragmented segments of the many influences shaping behavior that our formulations are frequently shattered by real events and by attempts to apply our formulations.

Re-Formation of the Self System during Adolescence

The study of natural reference groups is particularly important in understanding the individual-group-society relationship during *adolescence*. It can also indicate the motivational basis for the intensified interactions with age-mates that are so typical of adolescents in highly differentiated, casually patterned modern societies. With a decade or so of life behind him, the growing child starts to develop physically into an adult. The problems, events, and timing of adolescence vary enormously in different cultural and socioeconomic settings, but in nearly all societies, there are two sets of universals: (a) more rapid pace of growth involving profound biochemical as well as structural changes of the body, and (b) changes in the person's roles with accompanying shifts in responsibilities, activities, and ways of acting.

The changing body of the adolescent compels changes in his self concept. *Self concept* or *ego* refers to the constellation of attitudes that the person has formed relating his body and his individuality to other persons, groups, objects, values, and activities in institutions. Even if others were to take no note, the altering appearance of his body and its unaccustomed sensations tell the adolescent that he is changing. However, others *do* take note — his family, teachers, and friends expect new things of him; the mass media depict different ways of feeling and acting for his age group; he is expected to be more responsible and less dependent upon adults, at least in the conduct of routine activities and self care; he is expected to start to act, dress, stand, and walk in ways befitting the approach of adulthood. If the adolescent is to meet these expectations, he has to redefine relevant attitudes toward himself and others. In short, the fundamental psychological problem of adolescence is the general and important problem of forming and re-forming self or ego attitudes. Thus, adolescence is one of the best periods of development for studying an important problem in social psychology: attitude change.

In modern societies, however, the steps and procedures for attaining adulthood are by no means clear. For several years, the youth is neither child nor adult, neither dependent nor independent socially and economically. Adults are uncertain about the exact timing of steps and responsibilities he is to assume. Sometimes, when life has changed rapidly from when they were adolescents, adults offer guidelines so different from the paths open to the youth that the guides appear unacceptable. Furthermore, adult treatments are not consistent — the young person is treated as an adult one day, and subject to the restrictions and sheltered world of childhood the next. In short, to the extent that it is a prolonged transition with no clear and satisfactory procedures for gaining adult status, adolescence is a period of dilemma.

When faced with uncertainty and conflict about such central problems, any individual, of any age and at any place, searches actively for stable guideposts, some certainty, and some way out of the conflict. His choice of guideposts is, of course, contingent upon his own selectivity and capability at the time and upon the alternatives available and salient.

Today, the social schemes for school, community, and leisure encourage the adolescent's choice of guideposts from age-mates. The adolescent discovers that there are others in the same boat, and his social interaction with other adolescents becomes more intense, more frequent, and more significant than in childhood. Adolescents in the United States are encouraged in moving toward age-mates by the emphasis on social activities, by pressure from parents and other adults who want them to be "in," by school programs, and by the varied mass media that deliberately feed on appeals to youth. The actual movement toward age-mates is also symptomatic of a general shift away from their strong ties of dependence upon adults — for the time being, at least, the standards that *count*, the opinions that decide whether *I* am normal, average, superior, or inferior are those within the domain of adolescents.

Problems of being accepted and of being recognized by age-mates become major concerns. To be neglected, rejected, scorned, or ignored at a time when one's self identity is changing is a painful experience to be avoided at all costs. When coupled with an earlier history of insecure ties with family and other groups, such experiences may impel an almost frantic search to belong someplace with someone, and at almost any price. What becomes important during adolescence, therefore, is closely tied with day-to-day relationships with age-mates.

Experimental Demonstration. The shift in reference groups from family to age-mates was studied experimentally in our research program by Prado (1958), who compared judgments by children and by adolescents on the competence of their own fathers and their best friends in a simple task. Prado selected twenty-five boys between eight and eleven years old and twenty-five between fourteen and seventeen years old. In order to minimize the possibility of getting boys who had unusually poor relationships with their fathers, he chose only boys who consistently selected their fathers as their most preferred parent. He singled out the boy's best age-mate friend from sociometric data obtained at school.

Each boy came to the laboratory with his father and his best friend to perform the simple task of throwing a dart at a target. The task was arranged so that the exact score could not be determined by the subjects. Each boy judged his father's and then his friend's performance, using

103

scores from 0 to 24. The children and the adolescents were about equally accurate in their judgments, with an average error of 4.5 in judging their father's performance and an error of about 3.5 in judging their friend's performance.

The difference between errors in judging fathers and errors in judging best friends is an index of the comparative tendency to overestimate or underestimate performance by father and best friend. A positive difference would mean that the error in judging the father's performance was greater than that in judging the friend's and in the direction of overestimation; a negative difference would mean that the father's performance was *under*estimated, even when actual performance levels were taken into account. The findings were that children of eight to eleven years of age tended to *over*estimate their father's performance (mean difference, +2.35), whereas adolescents *under*estimated their father's performance compared to that of a friend (mean difference, −3.64). This experiment is one of several in our program demonstrating that systematic variations in a cognitive process (judgment, in this case) can provide precise indicators of the person's attitudes and affective ties.

Sociocultural and Ecological Characteristics of the Area

The consequences of the shift toward adolescent reference groups depend, in part, upon the facilities, the socioeconomic level, and cultural arrangements in which such reference groups function. These specific characteristics of the sociocultural setting are stimuli affecting the attitude and behavior of the subjects. We deliberately chose low, middle, and high socioeconomic areas of differing ethnic composition in order to reach generalizations common to all levels as well as to specify differences. Utmost care was taken to find measures to specify as exactly as possible the characteristics of the social areas in which the adolescents lived and moved. We relied especially on the Shevky-Bell Social Area Analysis (Bell, 1958; 1965; Shevky & Bell, 1955) to designate the ecological characteristics of each urban area. This analysis is based on the finding that the large number of separate items in census tract statistics tend to be intercorrelated and can, therefore, be reduced to three (or more) basic factors. Since certain items are better measures of these three factors than others, only a few of them are actually used in computing each of three indexes (Bell, 1965):

Index of SES	Index of Urbanization or Family Status	Index of Ethnicity or Segregation
Rent	fertility ratio	race
Education	women not in the labor force	nativity
Occupation ...	single-family detached dwellings	Spanish surnames

Shevky and Bell standardized scores on each of these three indicators according to the range in Los Angeles in 1940. This standardization makes it possible to compare the rank of areas in different cities, even though the basic yardstick (Los Angeles, 1940) was arbitrarily chosen. For example, Figure 1 gives the distribution of census tracts in our research up to 1964 according to socioeconomic status and family or urbanization status. The location of an area in such a matrix can be used in plotting behavioral or attitudinal data, indicating both the social class (low, middle, high) and degrees thereof.

By exploring and mapping facilities of each social area and, in some cases, conducting surveys among residents, we specified still further the character of the area as it presents itself to the members of natural groups. Although these data are clearly at the sociological level of analysis, they do provide a framework for the study of behavior far superior to the "boxcar" designation of social class, as John Campbell (1967) has called the gross measures typical in sociopsychological research. It does make a difference whether a lower-class area is composed of poor families living in small shanties or working-class families crowded into apartments.

The ecological arrangements and sociocultural characteristics of the urban areas proved invaluable in understanding many activities and behaviors within adolescent groups. For example, the spacious homes and many recreational facilities in an upper-middle-class area were associated with activities and attitudes toward space that differed strikingly from those in a poor, overcrowded neighborhood, where privacy was difficult to obtain. The conflicts among groups of adolescents in culturally segregated, underprivileged areas frequently centered about the limited space and facilities, whereas intergroup conflict in middle- and upper-class areas involved prestige and power, concerns related to space and facilities in only tangential ways. Again, the total absence of interest in athletics in one group of adolescent boys would have been difficult to understand without the knowledge that they lived in a social area inhabited predominantly by first-generation Mexicans of peasant origin, for whom sports in the North

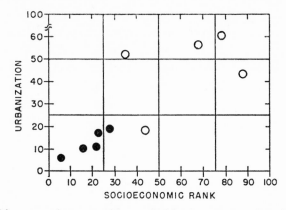

Figure 1. Urban areas from two cities studied in the program plotted according to socioeconomic rank and urbanization (termed family status by Bell). Each dot represents a census tract in which members of a given group lived. Each group was studied intensively. Axes indicate index numbers in Shevky-Bell Social Area Analysis. The index numbers are based on average percentages of several census measures (see text) which are standardized by weighting coefficients that adjust for the range of percentages obtained in extensive analysis of census tract statistics by Shevky and Bell, then converted to index numbers. Thus, index numbers can be compared between cities as well as within cities. Horizontal axis indicates socioeconomic rank. Vertical axis indicates increasing urbanization of family life-style (i.e., the higher on the axis, the higher the combined average for percentages of multiple-family, attached dwellings, of women working, and of low birth rate). Black dots indicate segregated areas with populations of ethnic status low on the social distance scale in the United States (Mexican Americans, in this case). Three areas of highest socioeconomic rank (upper right) housed segregated white populations, and intermediate areas indicated by white circles were mixed (not indicated in Shevky-Bell notation).

American sense were not normatively defined as activities associated with masculine identity.

Self Radius and Goals Prevailing within the Settings

The problem of integrating sociocultural data and behavioral data based on individual responses has plagued social psychology. For sociopsychological analysis, specification of major characteristics of the setting is necessary, but not sufficient. Certain aspects of the sociocultural setting have greater salience than others for individuals of a particular age level studied in their natural groups; literature on the subject shows that adolescents are particularly tuned to others of their own age. Accordingly, special emphasis is given in our research program to data on the bounds of what are acceptable and objectionable behaviors within the group, and on the goals prevailing in each sociocultural setting among representative samples of teen-age youth. Data from different areas can be compared to see what is common to them all and in what ways they differ. Data from Social Area Analysis provided the baseline for assessing values and goals prevailing among adolescents in the areas, and the data thus obtained, in turn, served as the baseline in assessing the attitude and behavior of specific individuals participating in small groups as members.

The Shevky-Bell indicators provided the basis for determining the social rank of areas where the self radius and goals prevailing among adolescents were assessed. Representative samples of high school students in the areas provided the data on the values and goals prevailing within each area, obtained through a questionnaire administered as a public opinion survey. The responses were treated as indicators of what youth in each area regarded as socially desirable reactions in the school situation. They permitted the estimation of what was valued, the level of goals set by adolescents in each area for the near and more distant future, and what were the minimum and maximum limits to the youths' own conception of success. The designation *self radius* refers to such limits as defined through various questionnaire items.

Impact of the Larger Society. Despite the rather sharply graded socioeconomic and ethnic stratification in the United States, there were marked similarities among the youth in different urban social areas. Though differing in appearance, specific styles of dress, and sometimes language, they all bore the unmistakable stamp of the larger culture, with its stress on individual success in private and material respects. The ingredients of individual success desired by nearly one hundred per cent of every sample of high school students included automobiles, comfortable homes, spending money, and at least a couple of hours a day "to do what I want to do."

Table 1 shows that responses of students in social areas of low, middle, and high socioeconomic rank in one city who responded to the question, "If I had my way, I'd like to live in a neighborhood in the X part of the city." It shows the percentage responding with the same location where they currently live, the "north side" of the city (which was undeniably the most comfortable), or some other location. As the table shows, the desire to stay in the same location decreased regularly from the high- to the low-ranking neighborhood, and the desire to move north increased (the high rank sample already lived there). If all had their way, almost all of them would be living in the north side of that particular city. The impact of the larger society was also apparent in other respects – notably, the great im-

Table 1. Area of Residence Desired by Male Adolescents Living in Social Areas of Differing Shevky-Bell Socioeconomic Rank and Ethnic Composition

Area of City Desired	High SES, Segregated, "Anglo"	Middle SES, Mixed		Low SES, Segregated, "Latin"
		"Anglo"	"Latin"	
Same as present	94.8%	59.6%	55.1%	34.8%
North[a]		33.3%	32.7%	53.2%
Other	5.2%	8.1%	12.2%	11.0%
Total N	81	113	56	127

[a] North was the area of residence of the high rank sample (chi-square test between "same" and "all other" responses was significant ($p<.001$, 3 df).)

portance assigned to at least a high school education and aspirations toward occupations of higher status.

Limits of Success Determined by the Setting. Since high school students are likely to give responses on a questionnaire that they consider socially desirable, it is interesting to see that what is socially desirable does differ according to socioeconomic rank of the area. As other research would lead us to expect, the absolute level of goals for future occupation, education, and income differed systematically from one area to the next. Our data yielded the additional finding that what was conceived of as "success" in these respects also differed. For example, Table 2 gives the average

Table 2. Reference Scales for Subsistence — Comfort and Goals for Weekly Income (1959) of Adolescent Males Living in Social Areas of Differing Shevky-Bell Socioeconomic Rank and Ethnic Composition

Response[a]	High SES, Segregated, "Anglo"	Middle SES, Mixed		Low SES, Segregated, "Latin"
		"Anglo"	"Latin"	
"Barely enough to live on"				
Median	$59	$55	$41	$35
C.L.	52–77	51–59	34–55	31–46
"To be really well off"				
Median	318	172	94	83
C.L.	239–455	142–207	78–150	70–100
"I want to make in 10 years"				
Median	229	142	98	85
C.L.	184–300	122–175	75–131	77–97

[a] Medians were computed because distributions of response were markedly skewed. C.L. refers to confidence limits of the median, which vary with both dispersion and number of cases. Despite overlap of confidence limits for response "barely enough to live on," a median test of the response distributions was significant ($p<.001$, 3 df).

(median) responses to a series of items concerning how much weekly income was needed to "just get along," was needed to be comfortable, and was desirable for him within ten years. Spanish-speaking samples were living in areas of low and middle socioeconomic rank. As the table indicates, the radius within which one sets his future aspirations differs from the high- to the low-ranking areas and is also affected by membership in a cultural minority deprived of opportunity. Psychologically, the adolescent's reference set established limits for the radius of the self in these respects.

Nevertheless, relative to their fathers' attainments and to their own conceptions of success, aspirations for upward mobility were common in middle and lower rank areas. Table 3 shows that approximately 40 per cent of the youth in low- and middle-ranking areas of one city aspired to occupational levels higher than their fathers'. This upward shift resulted from less desire for manual labor and greater desire to reach the upper occupational categories.

Table 3. Discrepancy between Adolescent's Desired Occupation and Father's Occupation

	Rank of Area		
Occupational Rank	High	Middle	Low
1. Highest professional, top managerial	− 0.8%	+ 2.5%	+ 3.0%
2. Professional, business, technical	−12.5	+20.3	+12.1
3. Lower professional, small business	+11.6	+10.6	+17.0
4. Sales and Clerical	+10.1	+ 8.6	+ 9.7
5. Skilled	− 7.6	−25.6	− 4.9
6. Semiskilled	− 0.8	−10.3	−22.6
7. Unskilled	0.0	− 6.1	−14.3
Percentage differing from rank of fathers' occupation	21.7%	42.0%	41.8%

Similarly, in response to inquiry about the amount of education "necessary for a person who wants to do the things I want to do" and the amount the subject himself desired, the aspirations in low, middle, and high areas differed systematically. The median was completing high school in low-ranking areas, some additional training in middle-ranking areas, and college in the high-ranking areas.

Greater Heterogeneity of Goals in Middle and Lower Rank Areas. The data on educational aspirations serve as a point of departure for another important finding: The values and goals that prevail among adolescents in lower- and middle-class neighborhoods are more heterogeneous than those in upper rank areas. Figure 2 consists of data on educational goals presented as a frequency distribution of the responses (number of years desired) for low, middle, and upper rank samples. The responses of youth in the upper rank area were most homogeneous, about 85 per cent desiring four or more years of education beyond high school. Although the typical response in the lower-class area is for a high school education, a sizable minority aimed at college. Certainly, there is little hint here of the supposed derogation of school that once was believed typical of the lower class. Similarly, the distribution in the middle rank area reveals considerable heterogeneity, even a bimodality.

In this and several other respects, the findings showed that youth in upper rank areas were most like-minded. Coupled with the fact that youth in such areas are also more frequently and extensively involved in formally

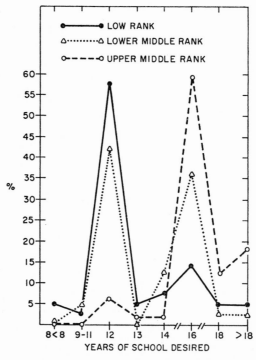

Figure 2. Percentages of adolescents in urban areas of different socioeconomic rank expressing educational goals for school attendance from eight or fewer years to more than eighteen years.

110

organized activities in school and community, this finding suggests that we might also expect to find less variety in the impact of age-mate reference groups in high rank areas. The intensive study of natural groups in lower and middle rank areas supported the conclusion that the impact of the group varied tremendously in terms of whether or not the group norms supported or were contrary to the values prevailing in and promoted by the high schools, law enforcement agencies, and other community agencies.

Intensive Study of Natural Adolescent Groups

The focal aspect of our program is the intensive study of natural groups. Since the program is sociopsychological, its procedures and data are concentrated on selected small groups and their individual members. Hence, the first requirement of the research design was the selection of clusters of teen-age boys (13–19 years) on the basis of their frequent and recurrent association in specified settings. Each group of four to twelve is studied intensively for periods of six to twelve months through a combination of techniques, including observation, behavior ratings by regular observers and independent observers, informal sociometric tests, and situational tests. The subjects are not aware that they are being observed. People *do* act differently when they know they are being watched and sized up; this is particularly true of adolescents, who are on guard in their relations with adults. Behaviors in the groups studied have included both socially acceptable and socially objectionable activities. However, groups were selected by their regular and recurrent association, and not by whether the members behaved properly or misbehaved. Thus far, we have completed the intensive study of four dozen groups in eight cities through the study cycle described below; we have partial data on a much larger number of groups.

The study is systematic in several respects. First, it is focused on obtaining data pertinent to hypotheses about the individual-group relationship. Second, it collects data on individual behavior or group members and on group processes in a systematic manner, using defined procedures in a definite sequence. Third, it seeks to relate these data systematically to the sociocultural and ecological findings, using the latter as the baseline to plot the attitudes and goals of group members and thereby viewing their conformity-deviation relative to others in their own area. Our major hypotheses and a string of auxiliary hypotheses in the present research were presented earlier (Sherif & Sherif, 1964). Here, we shall concentrate on two

111

major areas of theoretical interest: (a) To the extent that a set of norms is stabilized in regulating activities frequently engaged in, these norms become binding for the individual member; however, his conformity to them depends upon his status in the group. One indicator of stabilization of a set of norms is the extent to which members abide by them without threat of sanctions. (b) To the extent that a pattern of reciprocities is established as role and status differentiation among members, the behavior of the group members becomes more predictable. In other words, the more tightly knit the group, the more the interpersonal relations of group members and their attitudes toward outsiders become governed by it.

THE STUDY CYCLE

Our cardinal research strategy in studying groups is to accommodate the properties of every group as it actually forms and functions throughout the six- to twelve-month study cycle. We are acutely confronted with this issue from the very beginning as we start pinpointing a group for intensive study. First, an observer — a young adult college student or graduate student — is chosen to study one group. His first job is to master the instructions about steps and methods of observation (Sherif & Sherif, 1964, Appendix). In general manner, physical appearance, and speech, he has to fit into the area he is to study. Thus, a Spanish-speaking observer goes to a Mexican neighborhood, a Negro observer to a Negro neighborhood, an observer of upper-class background to a high rank neighborhood.

Next, he singles out a group — at first, *exclusively* on the basis of observed frequency and regularity of their association in the area (on street corners, in recreation areas, vacant lots, soda fountains, pool halls, skating rinks, and other hangouts). When he observes a minimum of four or five boys associating repeatedly, this cluster becomes a possible group for study.

The observer's first attempts are directed toward establishing his presence in the area as a harmless or neutral outsider in the eyes of the individuals. He has to develop a clear reason or pretext for being there, because there is a universal human tendency to categorize or place another person whom one meets for the first time. In other words, the observer himself is being observed, and in order to foster a categorization conducive to studying a natural group, he must be placed by the members as a harmless person who is *not* an authority figure or researcher or a reformer.

When, and if, he succeeds in establishing contact with the potential group, he begins intensive study. This consists of regular reports on each observation period, status rankings made on the basis of effective initiative and patterns of deference exhibited by each member, and ratings by an independent observer to cross-check the reliability of observer's ratings over a time span. Later in the study cycle, the observer's outside view of the status pattern is further checked against sociometric choices secured informally and privately from each individual to reflect perceptions from inside the group. The cycle also includes the observation of products peculiar to the group — recurrence of preferred activities, labels and nicknames, common practices and preferences, and reactions to cases of deviation.

The strength of group ties or solidarity (cohesiveness) of the group is checked through behavior of members in test situations and indicators of the effort they are willing to exert to associate with fellow group members. For example, such indicators are the alternatives chosen by the member when he is caught between staying with his group in a planned activity or getting away from it for a date, a family obligation, church, or school. Another indicator is the geographical spread of the members' dwellings, which reflects the effort and even sacrifice each has to make to associate with his fellow members rather than with others physically closer to his home. A third indicator is the frequency with which members know each others' whereabouts when they are *not* together.

Only after the observer has established close rapport with members, which usually takes several months, does he interview and directly question members to assess the natural history of the group's formation and to secure case histories of individual members in the neighborhood, including information about their homes, families, school records, and so forth. After a group is pinpointed, it usually takes from six months to a year to complete the cycle of study for it. The entire cycle adds up on the average to about a hundred observation periods for a single group.

The various data-gathering methods and procedures are introduced at a time appropriate to the degree of rapport developed between observer and the group members. We do not force upon members any direct questioning, interviewing, or other procedures which would be considered an imposition or an unwarranted intrusion into their privacy. Also, a special effort is made to keep members from becoming aware that the observer — who is hanging around as a harmless, well-wishing, older friend — is studying them and rating their behavior. Even with all of these precautions and a hands-off policy with regard to the planning and execution of group activities, the observer must maintain an uncritical attitude regardless of what they do. In spite of all such precautions, the establishment of rapport did not prove possible in every case. The reasons for such failures or for partial success are perhaps equally as important as the reasons for taking the precautions.

Groups are not formed for the benefit of outsiders to study them, including psychologists. They are not formed for a detached worker to reform them. They are not formed to tolerate criticisms, advice, and especially unfavorable evaluations by outsiders. They are formed in the process of interaction over a time span for satisfaction of members' common motivational urges, regardless of what these urges may be. Therefore, groups have designs, plans, and ends of their own, proportional to the extent that they are at odds with the established routines and channels, with other groups and institutions in their surroundings. They have secret designs and plans, and resist intrusions into their privacy, including intrusions by researchers and reformers. Invariably, in groups we have studied, the most difficult hurdle has been the initial period of secrecy and resistance to the observer, which he may not always overcome despite several months of persistence. When he did not, the study of such groups could not be carried through the entire cycle. We suspect that, even though the study cycle could not be completed, the walls of resistance and secrecy indicate tightly knit groups with highly stabilized organizations and binding commitments shared within the bounds of their particular membership.

THE OBSERVER BEING OBSERVED

In every case, for a period of several months the observer himself is under scrutiny by group members before they tolerate his presence in locations and spheres of activity which are the group's exclusive business. The critical phase toward establishing rapport is conceptualized as "the observer being observed." The members ask the observer point-blank who he is, what his connections are, and why he is hanging around; over the course of time, they check up on these points before they start opening themselves up — a luxury denied the observer himself at this initial phase of study. This period puts challenging and vexing demands on the patience, ingenuity, and skill of the researcher.

Gauging the degree of rapport attained at a given time should not be merely a matter of intuition. We have devised a combination of indicators of rapport for the timing of the several procedures in the study cycle.

These indicators include the observer's success in finding out the places where the group congregates when they are not in plain public view and their toleration of him in these places, the degree of intimacy of the activities they talk about freely or discuss in his presence, and the extent to which members permit or even welcome him into activities which they consider strictly private.

Why is degree of rapport important in decisions about research procedures that are appropriate at a particular time? It is not just a matter of whether or not one can collect data, for this is usually possible, but a matter of whether the data collected by a given procedure at a given time are *valid* as indicators of group properties and members' private attitudes. Strong emphasis should be placed upon the basis for developing rapport in order to secure valid and comprehensive data on group processes. This basis includes the assurance developed over time that the observer will not reveal private or secret activities to authorities and, in fact, has no connection with them. Such assurance is impossible for detached workers or others with official commitments to societal agencies, but it is necessary to ensure valid data about interaction among adolescents that is not deflected by an adult.

Patterns of Interpersonal Relationships within Groups

In this section, we shall concentrate on those indicators that are most useful in making accurate predictions about members' behavior. They can be accurately predicted because they are derived from the interaction process among individuals who really *count* in each other's eyes while they engage in activities that are important to them. These indicators include planning, discussion, and execution of actions that the members consider private or secret, and would not have exposed to any adult with authority. The first indicator is the member's position in the pattern of interpersonal relations of the group. The second pertains to the norms of the group. These two aspects of group process are closely related.

Our general finding is that associations of the sort we have studied are patterned affairs. Being a part of regular and recurrent interactions among age-mates who congregate of their own choice means regulating one's behavior with that of other group members. Over a period of time, the interactions among individuals become patterned and more predictable, so that they can be reliably studied in a variety of specific situations. Interactions follow various patterns, but the most predictive of behavior is the power dimension, as revealed by observers' ratings of effective initiative during interaction.

In our earlier studies of group formation and intergroup relations in summer camp settings, we had observed certain regularities in the patterning of interpersonal relations and power within a group (Sherif & Sherif, 1953; Sherif et al., 1961). It is significant that a similar pattern emerges in the perceptions of the members of a natural group, as indicated by their sociometric choices, and in the status ratings made by an observer over many observations when all members are present.

The member's position (rank) in a developing power structure is his status in the group, a differentiated aspect of his role that is defined in terms of the relative effectiveness of his actions in initiating, making, or approving decisions; coordinating interactions; and invoking sanctions for deviant actions by others. His status is further defined in terms of the evaluations of other members. The member's status, therefore, reflects a power dimension of role relations that is not identical with his ability to influence another's behavior in any situation at all. Nor is status identical with prominence, expertise, or the degree to which the person is liked. Power is manifested in situations where influence can be implemented with sanctions.

The referents of status and its significance in predicting members' behavior can be clarified by a diagram representing the process of group formation over time, as defined by the power or status dimension (Fig. 3). The status dimension in the diagram refers to the relative effectiveness of members in initiating activities over time in a variety of specific situations. At the top (Time *a*) are two collections of individuals with no previous history of interaction, but homogeneous enough socioculturally to hold other bases of differentiation constant. The circles indicate that, at this time, the individuals' relationships cannot be reliably ranked according to effective initiation of activities or of controlling interaction from one situation to the next; instead, the ratings of each person's effective initiative are different in various activities.

The course of status stabilization diagramed in the figure is based on the cumulative findings for six groups in a summer camp, formed experimentally by placing unacquainted, similar boys eleven to twelve years old in problem situations with highly appealing goals that could be attained only through coordination of action. The diagram represents two groups in the process of stabilization, to indicate that the particular pattern of organiza-

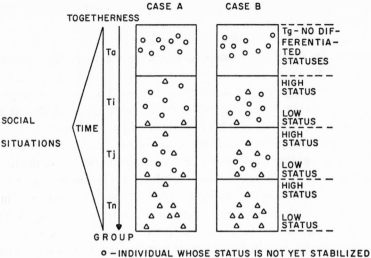

o — INDIVIDUAL WHOSE STATUS IS NOT YET STABILIZED

Δ — INDIVIDUAL WHOSE STATUS IS STABILIZED

Figure 3. Diagram of the formation and gradations of status structure over time from initial contact (top) to a stabilized group (bottom) in two illustrative cases. Stabilized positions (triangles) are based on agreement among several methods for ranking members according to their relative effectiveness in initiating plans and actions during prolonged interaction in naturalistic settings when facing problem situations of high motivational appeal. Note that Case A develops more vertical status levels than Case B, which has fewer differentiated status levels. Such differences were observed in the experiments that provided the data for constructing this diagram.

tion, the steepness or flatness of the hierarchy, and which individuals occupy what positions do not follow any set, predetermined form.

In the second frame at Time i the lowest and the highest positions are represented by triangles. The triangle stands for positions that can be reliably rated from one activity to the next and from one day to the next. The top position typically stabilizes earlier than other positions, followed by the lowest status positions.

At Time j in the figure, observers are able to agree on the positions most members occupy from one situation and from one day to the next, with the exception of the middle of the organization. Again, this is a typical finding for groups studied in both experimental and field conditions. In part, the continued flux in the middle ranks may reflect attempts by those in the middle to improve their standing or to align themselves with those of higher status. At Time n in the figure, the status relationships are stabilized; this is revealed both by all observers' agreeing on the status structure

117

and by members' perceptions of their relative standing, obtained through sociometric choices.

The speed or rate of stabilization diagramed in the figure will vary. In the particular camp experiments on which the diagrams were based, the groups stabilized within about a week while members lived together continuously and regularly engaged in highly appealing activities requiring coordinated action to attain goals within their own groups. Other investigators have reported discernible beginnings of group structure among individuals meeting in the same location for similar activities within three to five meetings lasting a few hours. Environmental events affect the rate of stabilization at least as much as internal relations of members. The stability achieved is sensitive to the introduction of new members, to changes in location and facilities, and to outside threat or emergency. Among the most solidary groups in our field study were those whose members had been forbidden by adults to associate, either as individuals or as a group. Thus, both a lower-class group of troublemakers and a high school fraternity ordered to disband were continuing their groups underground.

END ANCHORING

The general finding, then, is that regular and recurrent interactions among adolescents with common goal directions invariably become patterned through differentiation of member roles and status positions. Accordingly, the interactions among individuals become more predictable from one situation, one activity, and one time to the next, indicating recurrent regularities in attitude and behavior. The interactions are patterned in various ways, the dimension most predictive of behavior in important activities being the power dimension. *Who* gains *what* position remains an important problem for study.

One invariant in the stabilization of organization concerns the perception and judgment of the organization both by the members and by the observers. Theoretically, the important generalization about the stabilization process is that perception of the organization is polarized by the extreme positions at the top and bottom. Thus, in social organization, we are dealing with a general psychological phenomenon, namely, end anchoring. The end anchoring phenomenon refers to the finding in judgment experiments that extreme stimuli in a series (weights, frequencies, lengths, or position) are identified, learned, and judged more quickly and more accurately than intermediate stimuli. In serial learning and perceptual recognition in serial presentations, end anchoring occurs as a function of *order* of presentation, with the earliest and the last stimuli in the series serving to define the set (Harcum, 1967). De Soto and Bosley (1962) reported end anchoring in paired associate learning, in which subjects were required to learn names of unknown students paired with their college class (freshman, sophomore, junior, senior). Learning was faster both in number of errors and number of trials to perfect recall for the lowest (freshman) and highest (senior) classifications.

As Figure 3 shows, end anchoring was observed in the stabilization of six experimental groups. In the observation of several dozen existing groups of adolescents in natural field conditions, the observers' ratings of status over periods of time ranging from six months to a year were analyzed, with the invariant result that the ratings were more consistent for the highest and lowest status positions, with greater variability of rating in the intermediate ranks.

Figure 4 presents the composite findings on the ratings of a number of observers, each rating a different group. (Separate analysis for an individual observer of a particular group over time is presented in Sherif & Sherif, 1964.) The separate curves in Figure 4 represent averages in the vari-

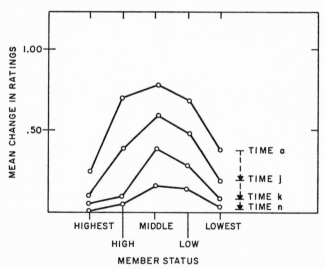

Figure 4. End anchoring in observers' judgments of status in natural groups of adolescents over time. Mean change in ranks assigned by observers according to observed effective initiative (status) during blocks of ten observation periods early in study cycle (Time *a*) to late in study cycle (Time *n*).

ability of ratings for separate blocks of observation periods (ten periods in each block) from the observers' initial encounters with the groups (Time a) to Time n, after they had observed for some months.

As Figure 4 shows, the most extreme representatives were recognized most readily and used as standards in judging others. It is important to note one difference from the end anchoring that occurs more typically in judgment or learning of a neutral series of stimuli. As a social structure, a group is affected by the superior anchor (high status) to a greater degree than a physical dimension would be. That is, the leader position exerts a greater anchoring effect than the bottom positions, both on the judgments of an observer and on promoting the stabilization of the structure (note that variability in rating lower positions is greater than that in rating higher positions). In general, the observer's variability in ratings decreases over time (Time a–Time n). This trend occurs, of course, when no drastic changes occur in the status structure during the time period.

As an important correlate of the end-anchoring effect, observers are more confident of their ratings at the extreme positions (see Fig. 5). The observers regularly rated their own confidence in the ratings they made on

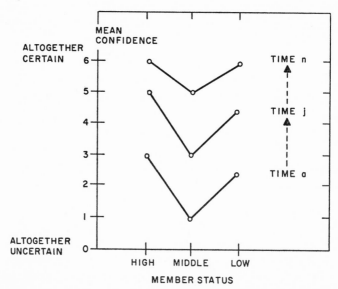

Figure 5. Mean confidence of observers associated with end anchoring in their judgments of status. Observers' self ratings of their own confidence from *altogether confident* (6) to *not at all confident* (0) when ranking members according to status in natural groups early (Time a) and later (Time n) in the study cycle.

effective initiative immediately following each observation period on a 7-point scale ranging from *altogether confident* to *not at all confident*. As Figure 5 shows, observers' confidence in their ratings increased over time, but was invariably highest at the extreme status positions, especially at the high end.

The finding that end anchoring is a general phenomenon of human judgment, both in laboratory experiments with neutral stimuli and in observations of group formation and group functioning, is all the more significant because it is not confined to trained observers. The same phenomena are detected in the participants' own perceptions of the group structure, as obtained through such sociometric questions as, Who gets things started? and Who gets things done? Consensus on choices is greatest for those in highest status positions (as independently assessed by independent observers) and those at the lowest positions (who receive few or no member choices on such items). In short, the stabilization of a hierarchical role and status structure is an invariant result of interaction over time among individuals facing common problems. Adolescent interactions are no exception: Choosing groups for study entirely on the basis of the recurrent, regular interactions among individuals, we have found that interpersonal relations among them are patterned and more or less orderly affairs, no matter how casual they may appear to the outsider.

The important result, from the psychological point of view, is that the status structure and the norms of the group provide a remarkably accurate basis for predicting the behaviors of individual members. This generalization has been tested using laboratory-like methods. The techniques are based on the general principle that a person's attitudes, expectations, and motives are revealed in his cognitive processes (e.g., in his judgment) when he faces an unstructured situation relevant to them. In other words, perception or judgment can serve as an indirect behavioral indicator of the person's attitudes, provided that the stimulus situation lacks objective structure in a relevant dimension. This principle had previously been demonstrated in experiments on judgments of future performance as affected by interpersonal attitudes (parents and children, husbands and wives, C. Sherif, 1947), by the mutual expectations of friends and rivals (Harvey & Sherif, 1951), by role and status expectations within small groups (Sherif, White, & Harvey, 1954), and by hostile attitudes toward a rival group (Sherif et al., 1961).

121

MULTIPLE EXPECTATIONS AS COGNITIVE INDICATORS
OF STATUS STRUCTURE

Earlier experiments suggested that members' appraisals of one another can serve as an unobtrusive or indirect method for studying status and role relations in a group. This possibility was explored further in a study by Koslin, Haarlow, Karlins, and Pargament (1968), which secured judgments on four different tasks from members of four groups. Specifically, these investigators asked whether differential expectations of performance by individuals with differing status in a group would be generalized across tasks and activities. They predicted that consistency in over- or underestimation of performance would be greatest for individuals occupying the highest and lowest status positions, with greater variability from one task to the next for judgments of members with intermediate status. This hypothesis was derived from the general principle of end anchoring.

In an athletically oriented camp for boys, four groups were observed over time, using the unobtrusive procedures described earlier. Each group consisted of six to eight boys between eleven and thirteen years of age; each group lived in a separate cabin ($N = 29$). The observer rated the effective initiative displayed by each boy in a variety of situations.

The four tasks used to tap expectations of performance were as follows: (a) A sociometric questionnaire administered to each boy individually on the pretext of improving the camp. (b) The height estimation test. Stick figures were presented to each boy with the instruction to imagine each figure as a member of his group, then to indicate where the top of his own head would reach on the figure. (c) The rifle task. Each boy shot one bullet at each of four targets placed fifty feet away. When a bullet hit the target, it disappeared. Other members observed his performance and recorded their judgments of his performance. (d) The canoe task. Each boy paddled from a bridge around a buoy and back to the bridge, whereupon other members recorded their estimates of the time required for performance. In the last two tasks (rifle and canoe), group members were already familiar with one another's proficiency before the estimates were obtained. The differences between estimated and actual performance were adjusted, therefore, to take account of level of skill.

Significant correlations were obtained between judgment variations in each pair of these four tasks and judgment variations in each task correlated with observers' ratings of status. The highest association between observed status and judgments was obtained when a multiple correlation was computed, using observed status as the criterion variable. The degree of relationship between performance expectations on the four tasks and observed status is indicated by the multiple r of .79 ($p<.001$).

Separate analyses of results for each group were made to evaluate the second hypothesis — namely, that end anchoring of judgments would be revealed through greater consistency (less variability) across the four tasks for members with highest and lowest status positions. Since the measurement units for the tasks were not comparable, the scores on each task were ranked within each group from highest to lowest. Then, the variation among each member's ranks on the four tasks was computed. This variance among ranks was correlated with status rank based on the observer's ratings using the statistic E (curvilinear association). Only the smallest group (Group II) in Figure 6 did not show a significant departure from linearity, and, even for that group, the curvilinear relation accounted for 65.6 per cent of the variance in the ranks.

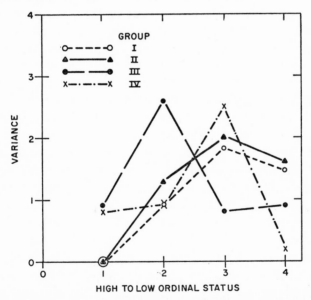

Figure 6. End anchoring in judgments made by members of natural groups I–IV of the performance by fellow members in four tasks (combined). Mean variance in ranks of members with differing observed status (high to low effective initiative on base line) when ranked separately on each of four tasks according to mean errors in judgments made by other members of their performance. Reproduced from Koslin et al., 1968, by permission of the American Sociological Association and the authors.

123

Koslin et al. concluded that their findings support the predicted relationships between sociological status in the group and member expectations on several independent tasks, suggesting a generalization of expectations for the member across tasks. However, this generalization is much greater — and hence expectations are more consistent — for high and low status ranks, as expected if end anchoring occurs in perception of group structure.

EFFECTS OF GROUP STABILITY AND MEMBER STATUS

Is effective initiative simply a function of the individual's attempts to respond adequately to the demands of the immediate situation, or do members' expectations on one another based on past interactions affect the exercise of power in a group? The answer to this question has important practical implications: for example, if one wants to influence an adolescent group by passing along information, which member will be most effective in influencing group members, one with high status or one with low status? An experimental study by MacNeil (1967) indicates that the answer to our question depends upon the *stability* of the group structure. Six natural groups of adolescent boys were selected on the basis of observations over periods from two to seven months. Using the reliability with which observers ranked each individual's status (top to bottom) as the primary criterion, several judges rated the stability of the groups, three being rated as high and three as low.

In each group, a member of high status and a member of low status were selected to be indoctrinated in an experiment with an arbitrary norm for judging highly unstructured situations (the autokinetic situation and the number of holes in a target made by a shotgun blast). In either case, the member was offered the chance to earn five dollars by substituting for a college student who had failed to appear for an experiment on the "human mind as a calculator." He served with a planted subject who distributed his judgments around an arbitrary mode and within a range much higher than was typical in the judgment situation. Since the judgment situations were highly unstructured, there was little difficulty in indoctrinating the group member with this arbitrary norm.

The question asked in the experiment was, What would happen when the indoctrinated member (either high or low in status) subsequently judged the same situation with other members of his group? Would the other members accept his judgments, knowing that he had previous experience in the experiment? MacNeil predicted that the answer would depend upon whether or not the group was a highly stable one and upon the status of the member.

Figure 7 shows that the effects of the indoctrinated members on judgments of other members of their groups varied markedly. The high status members of well-stabilized groups were very effective in influencing other members and maintaining the indoctrinated norm over five sessions, whereas low status members in the stable groups were scarcely effective at all — almost as if the other members had discredited their judgments before they started and evolved their own norms in the situation. In the less stable groups, the indoctrinated norm had a significant effect, regardless of whether the member was high or low in status. Here, the experimental situation itself became more important in determining the outcome: the fact that one of the members had previously served in the situation gave some credibility to his judgments, as indicated in the higher medians evolved by the less stable groups. On the other hand, in neither case was

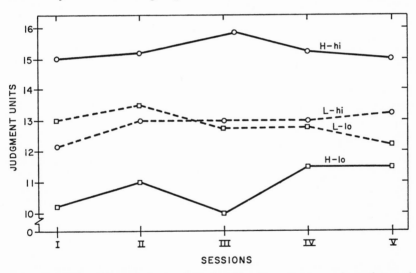

Figure 7. Median judgments in two tasks (combined) made by members of natural adolescent groups with high (H) or low (L) stability plotted for five sessions over time according to the status (hi or lo) of member who received highly arbitrary information in preceding session. Arbitrary information consisted of judgments of extraordinarily great magnitude made by a supposedly experienced subject. Ordinate gives medians for combined judgment scores on two tasks, adjusted for scale unit differences. The higher the score, the more effective was the member in inculcating the arbitrary judgments that he had acquired in the earlier session (not shown) with the "experienced subject." Reproduced by permission from MacNeil, 1967.

the member of a less stable group so effective in establishing and perpetuating the arbitrary norm as was the high status member of a stable group.

Conformity and Deviation of Group Members

The members of natural groups are "significant others" to one another. These reference groups constitute the significant and proper locus for studying patterns of conformity and deviation of their members. When we can locate an individual as a member of a reference group with specified properties, we have a basis for predicting what values he will conform to and which he will deviate from with little or no sense of guilt and with few or no pangs of conscience. More than that, if we know his position in the pattern of interpersonal power relations in that group, we have an effective basis for predicting the extent to which the values or norms of that group are binding for him personally, without threat of sanctions or other direct pressures from others.

Because much controversy has raged over the concept of "subcultural" variations in different neighborhoods and in different groups engaging in delinquent activities, it is important to note some features of the normative aspect of any group, whether delinquent or not. First, normative regulation is not to be found in all spheres of behavior or all activities. The convergence on customs and standardized outlooks by group members, with implied or actual sanctions for deviation, applies especially in matters of some consequence to the group and its members. Second, by their very nature, the norms of a group permit, even recognize, the play of individual differences. The norm defines a range or latitude for acceptable behavior, as well as a latitude of objectionable behavior to be met with disapproval or other sanctions. These two considerations become immediately obvious in actual observation of adolescent groups, whether delinquent or not.

CONFORMITY AS A FUNCTION OF STATUS

We have found that membership in natural reference groups is not binding to the same degree for all members, or in all matters. The latitude of acceptable behavior defined by a group norm, and the extent to which the norm itself is binding, have been determined through test situations contrived in the natural setting. The range, or latitude of acceptance, within which norms are binding depends both on the behavior in question and

126

upon the status of the individual in question. This generalization can be summarized briefly as follows.

The latitude of acceptable behavior, defined by group norms, varies according to the importance of the activity for the group. In matters affecting the identity, maintenance, and perpetuation of the group as a unit (such as *loyalty* in the face of outside threat or intrusion), the latitude for binding adherence to the group is restricted, and the bounds are sharply defined. Deviation in such matters calls forth strong and consensual sanctions from others, even separation from the group.

But even in matters of central and common concern, the norms are not equally binding for all members. The higher the individual's position, the narrower the latitude of acceptable behavior for him in such matters. The leader is expected to be exemplary in these respects, particularly in relations with outsiders. On the other hand, the leader is not placed under so great pressure to conform in matters of lesser importance, especially those occurring strictly within the confines of the group. For example, he can commit fouls in sports not to be tolerated from others, and he can offer insults not to be endured from those of lower status. On matters of minor importance, particularly those concerning the members when they are within the group, the leader's behavior varies within much broader bounds.

HOW BINDING ARE GROUP NORMS?

Of considerable import here is the question of how binding the group is for the individual adolescent when he is not in the presence of other members. Our observational data showed that once the individual has adopted the standards of his reference group, he is remarkably impervious to attempts by teachers, parents, or other age-mates to sway him from them. For example, one boy whose hair was considered a disgrace by his father and teachers and a joke by other teenagers refused to have it cut until members of his own group convinced him that his hair was a little beyond the bounds even of their norm.

This general question was examined experimentally by Pollis (1964; 1967), who selected members of natural groups and age-mates who were not friends to serve as experimental subjects. In the first session of the experiment, group members judged an unstructured stimulus (auditory) until they converged upon a common range and mode of judgment. Other subjects had the same experience either alone or in the company of an

127

age-mate with whom they had no previous relationship. In a second session, the group members were separated and placed with two other subjects who were comparative strangers. In this session, each of the three subjects already had a norm or reference scale for judging the situation, but each had a very different reference scale. Further, each subject differed with respect to the conditions in which he had formed his standard — either by himself, together with a comparative stranger, or with fellow group members.

Pollis asked the simple question, Who would be most influenced by the divergent judgments of others in the second session and who would, in turn, exert the most effect on others? The answer was that the individual who had evolved his own standard, individually, was most influenced by others and was least effective in swaying others; the group member who had formed his standard with fellow members adhered most closely to his norm and was more effective in influencing others. Those who had formed standards with comparative strangers were intermediate in both respects.

This simple experiment confirms a finding that appeared over and over in our observations of natural groups in the field: Proportional to the stability of a group, its norms are binding to members even when they are not face-to-face. As Pollis's experiment suggests so clearly, this adherence is not blind conformity but a product of interaction with high affect for people who really count for one another. Unless this emotional nexus is clearly understood, there is little chance for adequate analysis of the phenomena of conformity-deviation during adolescence.

Concluding Remarks

The properties of naturally formed reference groups place limits upon the procedures that the researcher can use and upon the sequence of their application, if he wants to collect valid data on adolescent attitude and behavior. Much more effort and patience are required than in laboratory research. But within the approach outlined here, measurement that is both precise and reliable comes within the grasp of field research. The precise methods of laboratory assessment can frequently be adapted for use in the much more complex arena of natural settings, and the laboratory, in turn, can be used effectively in conjunction with field research when the major essential variables are incorporated into the experimental design.

The enormously complex problems of the individual-group relationship during adolescence require the marriage rather than the divorce of theory and research methods from psychology and sociology. When small groups and their members are studied relative to their sociocultural settings, and the setting is studied relative to the group as a part of the setting, the dichotomy between the study of interpersonal interaction and the study of culture and social organization, which is still so prevalent, will disappear. What are considered the "psychological" and the "sociological" studies of social behavior will supplement each other, instead of being monopolistic preferences of their respective disciplines. On the psychological side, the contributions of particular individuals, for good or for evil, can be studied to any desired degree of elaboration within their appropriate stimulus settings. These settings are patterned affairs: They are the individual's reference groups and the sociocultural surround of which these reference groups are parts. The contribution of his personal skills and qualities to the behavioral outcome is not abstract — his unique individuality is seen in the ways he interacts with others in activities and situations that are important to the individuals in their concerted undertakings. These interactions are patterned affairs which provide the context for his own attitude and behavior, and which he, in turn, affects as an active participant. No theory of individual behavior can be adequate until these complex interactions are conceptualized, and until research operations appropriate to their study are developed and used in actual practice.

References

Bell, W. The utility of the Shevky typology for the design of urban sub-area field studies. *Journal of Social Psychology*, 1958, 47, 71–83.

――――. Urban neighborhoods and individual behavior, in M. Sherif & C. W. Sherif, eds., *Problems of youth: Transition to adulthood in a changing world*, pp. 235–264. Chicago: Aldine, 1965.

Campbell, J. D. Studies in attitude development: The development of health orientations, in C. W. Sherif & M. Sherif, eds., *Attitude, ego-involvement and change*, pp. 7–25. New York: Wiley, 1967.

De Soto, C. B., & J. J. Bosley. The cognitive structure of a social structure. *Journal of Abnormal and Social Psychology*, 1962, 64, 303–307.

Harcum, E. R. Parallel functions of serial learning and tachistoscopic pattern perception. *Psychological Review*, 1967, 74, 51–62.

Harvey, O. J., & M. Sherif. Level of aspiration as a case of judgmental activity in which ego-involvements operate as factors. *Sociometry*, 1951, 14, 121–147.

Koslin, B., R. N. Haarlow, M. Karlins, & R. Pargament. Predicting group status from members' cognitions. *Sociometry*, 1968, 31, 64–75.

MacNeil, M. K. Power of status in norm formation under differing conditions of group solidarity. Ph.D. thesis, University of Oklahoma, 1967.

Pollis, N. P. Relative stability of scales formed in individual, togetherness, and group situations. Ph.D. thesis, University of Oklahoma, 1964.

———. Relative stability of scales formed in individual, togetherness, and group situations. *British Journal of Social and Clinical Psychology*, 1967, 6, 249–255.

Prado, W. M. Appraisal of performance as a function of the relative ego-involvement of children and adolescents. Ph.D. thesis, University of Oklahoma, 1958.

Sherif, C. W. Variations in judgment as a function of ego-involvements. Paper presented at the meeting of the Eastern Psychological Association, Atlantic City, April 1947.

Sherif, M. *In common predicament: Social psychology of inter-group conflict and cooperation.* Boston: Houghton-Mifflin, 1966.

———. *Social interaction: Process and products.* Chicago: Aldine, 1967.

———, O. J. Harvey, B. J. White, W. R. Hood, & C. W. Sherif. *Intergroup conflict and cooperation: The Robbers Cave experiment.* Norman: University of Oklahoma Book Exchange, 1961.

Sherif, M., & C. W. Sherif. *Groups in harmony and tension.* New York: Harper, 1953; Octagon, 1966.

———. *Reference groups: Conformity and deviation of adolescents.* New York: Harper, 1964.

Sherif, M., B. J. White, & O. J. Harvey. Status relations in experimentally produced groups. *American Journal of Sociology*, 1954, 60, 370–379.

Shevky, E., & W. Bell. *Social area analysis.* Stanford, Calif.: Stanford University Press, 1955.

◈ BRIAN SUTTON-SMITH AND B. G. ROSENBERG ◈

Modeling and Reactive Components of Sibling Interaction

BEGINNING with Galton's assertion in *English Men of Science* (1874) that the eldest son is favored over his siblings because he is allocated more economic resources, is treated more as a companion, and is given more responsibility, birth-order studies have been a rampant if lowly weed in psychology for almost a century. A few preliminary remarks about some of these earlier as well as some of the more recent presystematic studies is in order — they add a flavor of romance to the field even if they don't add much to its clarification.

The early presystematic studies were devoted mainly to studies of the relations between ordinal position and eminence on the one hand, and ordinal position and various forms of deviance on the other. The latter studies of ordinal position and delinquency, alcoholism, schizophrenia, and so forth were, and still are, more or less inconclusive. But the bulk of the studies on relations between ordinal position and eminence have given the award to the first and the early born. By contrast, in folk and mythological literature, it has generally been the later born who have had preferred status — though the position is not quite so one-sided in that literature as Adler contended when he said that in fairy tales the youngest always wins. As a lighthearted check, for example, we scored Josef Scharl's edition of *Grimm's Fairy Tales* and found that half the tales including children were about *only* children. When tales with two, three, four, and seven children were compared, it was true that the later born always won more than any of the others, but there was an extreme disproportion in only the three-

NOTE: Many of the studies reported here were supported by Public Health Service grants MH-07994-01 through 05.

131

child family, where the third born won 90 per cent of the time. These three-child stories constituted only 20 per cent of all stories with children in them.

Irving Harris gives another twist to this diversion in *The Promised Seed: A Comparative Study of First and Later Sons* (1964), in which he suggests that most fairy tales are written by later borns for their own compensatory satisfactions. Harris's book, based on biographical accounts, is perhaps the best example of what we are calling presystematic literature. He speculates, for example, that Freud's attention to the oedipal position and Adler's to sibling rivalry arose from their own specific sibling conditions. First son Freud was concerned with the intimate relations of child and parent, fourth-born son Adler with the frustrations and jealousies of sibling rivalry. Another book of this same speculative character is Walter Toman's *Family Constellation* (1961); one of its more remarkable assertions is that better adjusted marriages are based on complementary sibling matches. Persons with opposite sex siblings have a better chance in marriage on this thesis, and there appears to be some slight evidence in its favor (Kemper, 1966).

Methodologically, the most important events in this field are Harold Jones's "Order of Birth in Relation to the Development of the Child" (1931) and Helen Koch's series of studies on siblings in the two-child family beginning in 1954 (1954; 1955; 1956a; 1956b; 1960). Jones emphasized the confusion resulting from the lack of controls for socioeconomic status, family size, family completeness, and the age of the mother, and Koch demonstrated the importance of the specific ordinal positions, the sexes of the siblings, and the spacing of them. The importance of the specific ordinal positions is illustrated by one of our own findings — namely, that although firstborns in general use higher power tactics than second borns — this is not true of the younger brother with an older sister. He appears to be more powerful than she — bribing, blackmailing, breaking and taking things, and making her feel guilty — tactics more usually favored by firstborns (Sutton-Smith & Rosenberg, 1968). Studies where the specific positions are pooled without regard to sex and contrasts made between all firstborns and all later borns obscure such exceptions. Effects of spacing are also ignored in most current studies, yet Koch showed clearly that the closer siblings, separated by one to two years, are more similar to each other and show less conflict than those separated by two to four years. And in a recent study of our own with college students, we have shown that close spacing results in higher cognitive performance for girls, and the wider spacing in higher cognitive performance for boys; we interpret this in terms of the facilitative effects of the close spacing on the development of the appropriate female sex role trait of dependence in girls and of the wider spacing on the development of the appropriate male sex role trait of independence in boys (Rosenberg & Sutton-Smith, in press).

Although Jones's methodological precautions had a deservedly depressive effect after 1933 on what had been a steady flow of inconsistent and unreliable studies, Koch's evidence has been largely ignored in the more recent studies prompted by Schachter's *The Psychology of Affiliation* (1959).

Theoretically, this is a field of much loose speculation, many tacit assumptions, and few explicit or comprehensive formulations. In attempting to bring some clarity to our work in this field we have found it helpful, as have others (Kammeyer, 1967), to focus on the particular classes of interaction in which the siblings find themselves. It is our contention that a focus on such classes of interaction has promise of moving a step closer to an operational understanding of how the rather distant relations between the status variable of ordinal position and the observed differences in sibling cognitive performances and personality traits actually occur, and can also lead to some overview of the types of developmental patterning that occur in families of different sibling-parent constellations.

The studies discussed here can be placed in three groups: (a) those focused on *parent-child* interactions, in which the major dependent variables have been achievement and affiliation; (b) those concerned with *child-child* interactions, in which the major dependent variables have been chiefly those of sex role traits and power; and (c) those in which some attempt has been made to consider *patterns of interaction* or constellations involving the whole family. Our research has fallen chiefly in the last two categories, and was carried out at Bowling Green State University during the years 1962–1967.

Within each of these broad classes of interaction, we have also found it useful to divide the interaction itself into two aspects. In each interaction there is both the role of the other person and the subject's own response. In the interaction a sibling may vicariously model the role of the other person while he is at the same time reacting to it. These can be spoken of as the *modeling* and *reactive* components of the interaction. A central question raised throughout the rest of this paper is whether the depend-

133

ent variables examined can be considered to be variables generalized from either the modeling or reactive components of the original classes of interaction. Although it is possible to seek beyond these components for more remote levels of interpretation — as is often done, for example, with concepts such as identification, power, facilitation, and assimilation — and although we shall refer occasionally to such concepts, the most useful preliminary step is to concentrate on these more immediately observable aspects of the social interaction itself.

In our research, we have looked for several things. We have been trying to discover how firstborns both react to and model after their parents but, at the same time, model after and react to their younger siblings. The same modeling and reaction occurs for the later born, but the position seems to be somewhat different. Unlike the firstborn, the later born do not seem to be caught between the two systems; instead, they appear to be interacting within several collateral but similar systems — that is, they are modeling and reacting to older siblings on the one hand, and to parents on the other.

Parent-Child Effects

ACHIEVEMENT

It is historically appropriate to begin with the empirical, Galton-derived tradition which seems to show that firstborn children are overrepresented in terms of eminence, college attendance, and achievement (Altus, 1966). Unfortunately, there are methodological difficulties in assessing the degree of overrepresentation that have seldom been attended to. Bayer has shown that the vital statistics indicate that the proportion of children firstborn any year has varied from around 30 per cent in the 1920's to a peak of 43 per cent in 1942. It stayed high until around 1947 and has descended ever since, coming down again to 27 per cent in 1960 and presumably to a much lower level at present, judging by the dropping birth rate. None of the recent studies of overrepresentation in scientists, college attenders, and so forth contrasts firstborns with their own baseline twenty or sixty years beforehand (Bayer & Folger, 1967).

An alternative approach is to compare subjects from the same families. The most adequate study, a national survey by Bayer (1966) involving approximately ten thousand subjects and comparing those attending and not attending college in relation to family size and birth position, has shown that the last born are about as likely to go to college as the firstborn from families of the same size and socioeconomic position. Further, within each socioeconomic level, only children are more likely to attend college than are those who have siblings. Least likely to get to college are children of an intermediate family position. Thus, any gross comparisons of first versus later borns will appear to elevate the firsts by combining them with the only children and will appear to depress the last born by combining them with the middle born. In the total literature on ordinal position there has probably been more effort wasted on explaining the relative distinction of the firstborn than on any other single ordinal condition. Bayer's data shifts the burden of such speculation to the special position of only and middle children. The most parsimonious thesis might well be that the gross differences between performances of only and of middle children have their basis primarily in the quantity of interactions occurring between parents and children, with the middle borns getting least and the only children the most. Such gross differences in interaction could support any or all of the various reinforcement, modeling, and identificatory contingencies spoken of at great length in the literature.

AFFILIATION

Schachter's key study, *The Psychology of Affiliation* (1959), presents the only near-systematic theoretical framework in the sibling literature. Judging by the various studies on affiliation and conformity that have derived from this work, it would appear that social comparison theory, which suggests that humans have a drive to measure themselves against others around them, is particularly appropriate for onlies and firstborns. In studies by a number of investigators involving situations of anxiety or uncertainty, onlies and firstborns have more often sought to affiliate with or conform to others. Or to state matters more precisely, in nineteen experimental studies involving affiliation measures, there have been fifteen in which a predicted ordinal effect has been confirmed; and in eighteen experimental studies involving conformity measures there have been eleven confirmations (that is, 26/37) (Sutton-Smith & Rosenberg, in press). However, it should be added that results for females in conformity studies have been predominantly negative (two successes out of seven).

When the reasons for this moderate degree of success in these studies are analyzed, however, the picture is far from simple. There is little uniformity across the studies. Do the onlies or firstborns affiliate because they are initially more anxious or because they have higher need affiliation?

Within the experiment, is it fear, or uncertainty, or solitariness that induces the responses? Do these responses involve anxiety reduction, emotional comparison, cognitive comparison, or simply the seeking for similar others? Within the conformity experiments, do the onlies and first borns conform because they begin by being more anxious, or uncertain, or dependent? Within the experiment, are they more responsive to normative influence, or is their conformity due to the character of the judgments (perceptual or conceptual) that they are called upon to make, or is it due to the character of the reward? Drawing upon the details of the thirty-seven studies, there are both positive and negative answers to most of these questions.

A more important criticism of these studies, however, is that they do not give any consideration to the representative character of the experimental situation. These experiments are miniature social situations, and one of the most significant conclusions to be derived from them depends upon the logical parallel to be drawn between them and other social situations. For example, none of the studies contains any controls for the experimenter as a variable, but the corpus of birth order studies strongly suggests that there are birth order differences in responses to adult power figures. Lack of control for the experimenter as a variable introduces the strong possibility that the consistent results across the varying conditions are brought about by the subjects' special and differential attitudes toward the experimenter (for example, their willingness to volunteer) rather than the explicit experimental conditions. Again, in the conformity studies, controls are not exercised for the fact that accomplices in the Asch situation are peers, despite strong evidence that birth orders differ in their acceptability to peers. On both these counts, then, experimenters and peers treated as neutral conditions in studies done so far may have affected the results in ways outside the investigators' control.

Still, in over two thirds of the studies there were ordinal position differences, and these results have to be reckoned with even if the changing contingencies across the experimental studies render interpretation difficult. Speculating tentatively on the origin of such differences, Schachter presented the opinion that in early childhood firstborns had been taught to associate the reduction of pain with the presence of others. The inexperienced mother rushing to the baby at every whimper, ready to interpret every burp as a death rattle, quickly conditioned the youngster to expect social solace in the presence of pain, fear, or uncertainty. As the children grew older and increased the magnitude of their own instrumental responses, they sought out other persons when in states of anxiety and uncertainty. Most of the investigators in the thirty-seven studies mentioned have taken for granted this infant-deterministic thesis of Schachter's. We can, therefore, raise the question whether there is indeed any evidence that mothers treat infants differentially by ordinal positions. Most self-report data are positive. More importantly, in one observational study (Lasko, 1954) and two experimental studies (Cushna, 1966; Hilton, 1967), the answer is also positive, though what the parents actually do with the children varies across the studies, they exert more pressure upon, or are more inconsistent with, or expect more of the firstborn. The observational or experimental studies of firstborn preschool children also indicate that, as expected, they are more dependent or help-seeking (Cushna, 1966; Gewirtz, 1948; Hilton, 1967; Schachter, 1959). Most of the parental report studies are of the same import. To this point, therefore, there is good reason for believing that the results in the college level experimental studies and the results in these experimental and observational studies of children may be connected in the way Schachter suggests.

Once we proceed beyond the preschool years into the childhood studies, however, the results are less consistent (Gilmore & Zigler, 1964; Koch, 1955; Walters & Ray, 1960). Some reconciliation of the different studies can be made if, instead of treating all the ordinal positions as if they were alike, the specific sibling positions are dealt with separately. To date, this has been done in only three studies of the eight positions in the two-child family — Koch's with six-year-olds (1955), Sampson and Hancock's (1967) with adolescents, and Bragge and Allen's (1966) with college students — but with remarkably consistent results. What these studies show fairly clearly is that some firstborns and some second borns fit the expectations across the age levels, but some do not. If both children are boys, for example, the same sex pair match expectations — that is, firstborn boys with younger brothers (M1M) conform, affiliate, or are dependent, and their younger brothers are not (MM2). Girls in an opposite sex pair also match expectations — the girl with a younger brother is conforming (F1M), and the girl with an older brother is not (MF2). But girls with same sex siblings and older boys with opposite sex siblings do not match expectations drawn from the Schachter hypothesis. It is clear from these results that some of the positive and negative results in the 37 studies may well have been produced by haphazard sampling across the eight very different ordinal positions.

The question is, Why do the preschool data on gross ordinal position differences largely support the Schachter thesis? and why are the child and adult data inconsistent? Both Koch and Bragge and Allen offer interpretations for their data which imply that as children become relatively independent of their parents at the end of the preschool period, they come increasingly under the influence of siblings and peers. For example, the second-born boy (MM2), who, as a second-born infant, is relatively nonconforming, remains nonconforming if he has an older brother and models after him (nonconformity being more typical of the male sex role), but if he has an older sister and models after her, (FM2) becomes more conforming (conformity being more typical of the female sex role) and no longer reacts as a second born should — that is, with less conformity. Likewise, the second-born girl, who should be nonconforming, stays nonconforming if she has an older brother to model after (MF2), but becomes more conforming if she has an older sister (FF2). Similar analyses can be made for the other sibling positions.

We should like to make several important points — both methodological and theoretical — about these three studies. First, if the investigators had not taken the precaution of studying the subjects' specific ordinal positions, these results would not be available. Second, an infant-deterministic thesis which does not take into account the cultural scheduling of contingencies (in the present case, the effect of older siblings on the sex role development of younger siblings) provides an oversimplified explanation for sibling differences, although it may hold up fairly well in the early years before these contingencies have important influence. Third, and of greater significance, the analysis above suggests that conformity or affiliation have different functional significance for different siblings. Even when the responses are the same, the motives may be different. Thus, an M1M may conform in the experimental situation because he has reacted to his parents in this way, whereas an FF2 may also conform, but because she is modeling the sex role traits of her older sister. In the terms of game theory we should say that their similar responses to the experimental situation have a different utility.

In socialization theory, it is usually supposed that early borns get to college more often because they model after their parents or are urged on by them (modeling or reinforcement). However, a speculative explanation can be drawn from their reaction to parents and teachers throughout childhood. For example, given the greater interaction between early borns and parents, and these children's greater dependency, some of Hilton's recent experimental work becomes relevant. She found that firstborns' mothers were more inconsistent, interfering, and extreme, and she suggested that, as a result, firstborns become more dependent on external social criteria (1967). In a subsequent experiment, she found that (regardless of ordinal position) highly dependent children performed productively when adult figures made inconsistent demands upon them. Nondependent children were merely confused by such inconsistencies (1968). This adds up to the speculative view that early borns become more eminent and achieving because they are dependent subjects who react productively to inconsistent demands (for infants who are already dependent, inconsistency is a form of partial reinforcement). In these terms, early borns generalize their dependence-productive reaction to parental inconsistency into a similar reaction when they are with teachers. It is not hard to believe that most teachers are both inconsistent and interfering and also satisfy dependency needs. Sutton-Smith, Roberts, and Rosenberg (1964) have shown that female firstborns predominate among teachers, which suggests that we are in the midst of a propitious cycle. This thesis might explain more adequately the multiple cases of early borns who go to college, but neither have parents who went to college nor were expected to go themselves.

To this point, then, we have suggested that we can consider the achievement and affiliative performances as generalized from the reactions of only and of some firstborn children to their parents.

Child-Child Interactions

With child-child interactions, each child both models after the other and reacts to him. One way to test for such influences is to contrast subjects with like sex siblings and subjects with opposite sex siblings.

SIBLING SEX EFFECTS

Self-report data, including studies with occupational, clinical, recreational, and masculinity-femininity inventories, show fairly clearly that a subject's preferences are more like those of the opposite sex if he or she has an opposite sex sibling (Brim, 1958; Koch, 1956a; Rosenberg & Sutton-Smith, 1964a; Sutton-Smith et al., 1964; Sutton-Smith & Rosenberg,

1965). Here, presumably, is an example of modeling. The data on abilities are also consistent in showing that girls model after male siblings, achieving higher quantitative scores when brothers are present, but that boys are not affected comparably by female siblings (Altus, 1966; Koch, 1954; Rosenberg & Sutton-Smith, 1964a; 1966; Schoonover, 1959). The interesting contrast is that on sex role variables males and females model after each other, but on cognitive variables only the females model.

A more striking example of the effect of two siblings upon each other is provided by our comparison of various patterns of father absence and sibling presence (Sutton-Smith, Rosenberg, & Landy, 1968). Using college entrance scores of siblings in two-child families, we compared those whose fathers had been present with those whose fathers had been absent from their birth to five years old, from five to ten years old, and from ten to fifteen years old. When fathers were absent during the children's fifth to tenth years, scores were significantly depressed, but as might be expected, firstborns were more affected than second borns, and boys with sisters were more affected than boys with brothers. The scores of a boy with a brother (first or second) were not significantly depressed by the father's absence — the father's effect on the cognition of his sons was apparently counterbalanced by the sons' ability to model after each other. In general, the father's absence had less effect on girls, except for the girl with a younger brother, whose scores were depressed by his absence. The most puzzling finding was that only girls' (those without siblings) scores were depressed by father absence, but only boys' scores were not. Although this finding is consistent with reports on the relative femininity of such boys and relative masculinity of such girls, the implication seems to be that in this oedipal triad, each is modeling after the opposite sex parent, not after the same sex parent, as we should expect.

Using time sample observations on one hundred same and opposite sex siblings in school settings, we (Sutton-Smith & Rosenberg, in press) have been able to establish that second-born subjects with opposite sex siblings initiate more interactions with opposite sex peers (initiating interaction with same sex peers does not differentiate between groups). Of course, we do not know whether such second borns generalize these interactions from the family to opposite sex peers because they are themselves more like the opposite sex (having modeled after it) or because they are used to reacting to the opposite sex. More molecular observations of the sex role character of the interaction sequences might throw some light on the modeling or reactive components of their behavior.

In most of these data, the younger are more affected by the older than vice versa. An older sibling has more effect in making the younger like him or herself. Thus, the boy with an older brother is generally the most masculine of boys, and the girl with an older sister the most feminine of girls. Likewise, the boy with an older sister is the most feminine of boys, and the girl with an older brother, the most masculine of girls. As far as this child-child interaction of second borns and sex role data is concerned, modeling seems to be the most important process.

By contrast, the data on firstborns in these child-child interactions would seem to indicate that the older children react to the younger — not by modeling after them, but by intensifying their modeling after the parents. The firstborns seem to be affected primarily by the way the later born interfere with their relationship with the parents — at least they do at age six in the Koch data (1956b). Her study shows that the sex of the intruding younger infant has a profound effect on the older sibling, making him more likely to assume the sex role characteristics of the parent whose sex is opposite to that of the infant. Hence, a boy with a younger brother shows an increase in feminine traits; a girl with a younger sister an increase in masculine traits; and so forth.

In each case it might be argued that the younger sibling heightens the importance of the opposite sex parent for the older sibling. Whether rivalry is the major motive, as in the classic view, we do not know, though it seems a reasonable interpretation. At present we wish merely to suggest that the older child models after the parent, not just because the parent is there, but also because of his reaction to the younger sibling.

There are other data to show that the principle of reacting to a sibling by modeling after the opposite sex is a fairly general principle (though sometimes this opposite is of the sibling's own sex role, and sometimes of the other sex role). Thus, a boy with two sisters as compared with a boy with one sister (Rosenberg & Sutton-Smith, 1964a), and a father with two daughters as compared with a father with a daughter and a son or as compared with a father with two sons, make significantly *lower* feminine self-reports on the Gough Scale of Psychological Femininity, not *more* feminine self-reports, as the bulk of the sex role preference data would have led us to expect (Rosenberg & Sutton-Smith, 1968). (The father's femininity scores as a function of the sibling constellation are shown in the accompanying tabulation.) Furthermore, our observational study has indicated that whereas the boy with one sister during preadolescence both reports to be more like that sister and also interacts more with girls in the classroom, the boy with two sisters reports being more masculine and does not interact any more with girls in the classroom than does the boy with two brothers.

Family Structure	N	Gough Femininity Score
Two daughters	90	16.55
Son and daughter	70	17.46
Daughter and son	49	17.00
Two sons	40	18.55

Yet another case is that of a developmental change from modeling after the other sibling to reactive modeling of opposite traits. This occurs in the boy with an older sister (FM2), who is the most feminine boy on most measures throughout childhood. When his elder sister leaves home to go to college, however, his femininity scores no longer correlate with hers. Furthermore, Leventhal has shown that during their own college years, these same boys, although continuing to have a more feminine level of anxiety than boys with brothers, nevertheless are superior in their ability to do chin-ups and to swim as judged by tests in physical education classes; they also show a greater interest in such pursuits as hunting and mechanical activity (1966). Again in earlier work it was found that mother dependent boys during preadolescence gave themselves higher scores on masculine self-report inventories (Sutton-Smith, 1965). In all these cases, the males appear to react to flower power by more intensively modeling male sex role traits. Perhaps, as in much other sex role data, males do their vicarious modeling from extrafamilial sources — heroes of culture, television, baseball, and so forth. Various concepts such as compensation, negative identification, adaptation level, and family sex role balance have been advanced to explain processes like these. Whatever the source, the fact of such reactive modeling appears to merit more careful attention.

POWER

Although there are various theses with respect to the power relations among siblings, the simplest thesis would appear to be that those who are larger will have more power and will exercise it. Older siblings will react to the weaknesses of their younger siblings by using more powerful tactics. Males will likewise use more powerful tactics than females. In a series of studies involving children and college students we have recorded the responses of members of the eight two-child families to a forty-item power tactics inventory. Subjects rate their own tactics and those of their siblings on a five-point scale. There is consensus among siblings on about 25 per cent of the items at both child and adult levels. For the children, it is clear that the greatest consensual agreement is that firstborns are perceived both by firsts and seconds as more bossy: M1M ($p<.001$), F1F ($p<.001$), F1M ($p<.05$), M1F ($p<.25$). Of similar consensuality is the tendency of seconds to show what is presumably a lower power reactive procedure of appealing to others outside the sibling dyad for help — crying, pouting, sulking, threatening to tell tales, or using prayer. Seconds in category MM2 ask other children ($p<.02$) or complain to the parent ($p<.10$); in FF2 ask parents for help ($p<.01$) or tell tales ($p<.05$); and in MF2 ask parents for help ($p<.05$), complain to parents ($p<.001$), or ask other children ($p<.05$). Crying and pouting is also common in MM2 ($p<.01$), FF2 ($p<.05$), and MF2 ($p<.01$). Only the boy with an older sister does not seek help outside the dyad, nor does he sulk or pout. Apparently, the younger brother with an older sister does not show the same degree of powerlessness as the other second categories, a finding which replicates a difference for this boy in an earlier study (Sutton-Smith, 1966). His subsequent display of physical power during the college years is perhaps presaged by this power experience within the family, though, as we have seen, modeling after an older sister throughout childhood, he appears more feminine on most measures.

Physical power tactics appear to vary with sex. Thus, beating up, hitting (M1M, $p<.01$), and wrestling and chasing (FM2, $p<.05$) are ascribed to boys. But scratching and pinching (FF2, $p<02$; MF2, $p<.02$) and tickling (F1M, $p<.05$) are ascribed to girls. The direct physical power of M1M and FM2 apparently has a strong effect on their siblings, since these siblings are the only ones who score higher on getting angry, shouting, and yelling (MM2, $p<.05$; F1M, $p<.05$). The polite and perhaps strategic techniques of explaining, asking, and taking turns are attributed only to firstborn girls (F1F, $p<.05$; F1M, $p<.01$).

There is a close parallel between these types of power and Koch's report of quarreling among six-year-olds of the same sibling positions (1960). Reports on the more socialized aggression of older siblings as compared with the more direct anger and physical aggression of later borns are of similar import. In the present data the tactics are mainly those found in any pecking order or social structure, though a few of them suggest parental modeling. Thus the older girls' use of explaining, giving reasons, and asking may perhaps be generalized from vicarious modeling after their mothers, with whom they have more frequent relations than do the second borns. Again, "excluding" and "taking turns" might perhaps be regarded as "affiliation" strategies, assuming that those firstborns who are affiliative learn to develop such devices. With the exception of these possible examples of parental modeling we have a situation to be explained primarily in terms of the members' reactions to each other (Sutton-Smith & Rosenberg, 1968).

The inventory results with college students were similar to those with the children so we shall not repeat them here. There is, however, considerable consensus across these age levels. Whether this consensus is due to power stereotypes across age levels or to the facts of sibling interaction is not clearly established, although we prefer the latter view. Our best evidence is from a role-playing experiment (Sutton-Smith & Rosenberg, in press). In the college data the firstborn had usually been seen as bossy and the later born as bothersome, so in the role-playing experiment, F1F and FF2 alternated in playing bossy and bothersome roles and in observing other F1F's and FF2's playing these roles. Without knowing which was which, the firstborns generally identified most with the bossy role, and the second borns with the bothersome one.

The college power tactics inventory we used was derived from our earlier content analysis of an open-ended questionnaire in which students gave answers not only about their tactics as siblings but also about their behavior toward parents and their parents' behavior toward them. The value of some of these results is that they present evidence about the context of parent-child power interactions within which sibling-sibling interactions take place. Thus, if the assumptions are made that parents are more powerful than children, males than females, and firstborns than second borns, then a scale of power types can be developed. At the high end of such a scale are such techniques as command, physical restraint, making the other feel guilty, making the other feel obligated, glorifying the job to be done, depriving of privileges, and reprimanding. At the low end are sulking, prayer, wishful thinking, claiming illness, pleading and whining, appealing for sympathy, appealing to parents, threatening to tell, teasing, and harassing. In the middle is a no-man's-land where those of high or low status may resort to reason, explanation, flattery, bargaining, bribery, trickery, blackmail, anger, and shouting. Several conclusions can be drawn from the results of our administering this inventory:

a. In these terms only children have parents who both are perceived as more similar to each other in the array of power techniques that they use and are using more high-power techniques than parents in two-child families. In two-child families, the mother and father are more differentiated, with the father using more high-power and the mother more low-power techniques. We may conclude that the children are more powerful vis-à-vis parents in the two-child family.

b. Within the two-child family, females report using more differentiated high- and low-power techniques with mothers and fathers than do males. Males report using trickery and appeal to the fact that they are boys with both mothers and fathers, whereas girls report pleading, whining, and appealing for sympathy with the mother but reasoning, persuading, and giving rewards to the father.

c. Both sexes perceive the opposite sex parents' using an appeal to sex (do it because you are a girl/boy), and the same sex parents' using a greater variety of pressure tactics. Boys see their fathers as using physical restraint and blackmail, and girls see their mothers as reprimanding them, glorifying the job to be done, making them feel guilty about it, making them feel obligated to do it, and appealing for their sympathy. Mothers, like daughters, also use a wider range of power techniques.

d. As the literature would lead one to suspect, firstborns report many more differentiated kinds of influence upon and influence by parents than do second borns. The seconds, on the contrary, suffer a more homogeneous administration of high-power techniques. In the face of the superior power of both parents and firstborn, the second born's most pronounced technique is that of withdrawal, a finding reminiscent of Schachter's work on affiliation (1959).

We favor the view that the simplest way to look at these sibling power differences is in terms of the dominance hierarchies to be found in all groups, animal or human. Koch's data for six-year-olds and our own data for preadolescents and college students show sufficient similarity to justify the view that we are concerned here with interactional structures of considerable stability. Developmentally speaking, these power differences should have a considerable effect on the emergence and stabilization of power responses, simply because they are of such an enduring character. This does not mean, however, that the responses generalize in any simple fashion. The second born, in particular, not only have their low-powered reactions to the firstborns' power (anger, appeal for help), but they may also vicariously model the character of that power from the firstborns and perhaps apply it more frequently elsewhere because they have suffered from it so intensively in the home. In at least one study we found that non-firstborns mentioned as their best friends those whom they could boss, whereas the firstborns mentioned as their best friends those who bossed them (Sutton-Smith, 1966). Here each sibling reversed rather than repli-cated his sibling role. Or perhaps more truthfully, the firstborns general-ized their subordinate reactions to parents, and the secondborns modeled the power they had observed the firstborns practicing. Still, these re-sponses were supposed to represent what these subjects did in play with their best friends, and they may have represented fantasy as much as a reality. The point is that although sibling power differences are enduring, no easy generalization is possible from the sibling power structures we have documented to other social settings.

Constellations

There are no very explicit statements about expected constellations across different types of family-sibling arrangements for different varia-bles, although there are some suggestions to be derived from balance theo-ries such as those of Parsons and Levi Strauss. Our own power data seem to imply that the balance and character of power relations change with family size. Koch's diverse data on six-year-olds appear to show that in the two-child family there is some tendency for children and parents to di-vide up the spoils — that is, for there to be complementary alliances. But none of this material is very clear yet.

FIRSTBORNS

In the previous two sections we have looked at firstborns in relation to parents (achievement and affiliation) and firstborns in relation to second borns (sex and power). Here we shall attempt to fit each of these classes of interaction into some larger family patterning.

We have suggested that early borns are more likely to react to parents with dependency and productivity. They are also likely to react to later borns with high power tactics and with modeling of later borns' character-istics, though in a relatively diluted way. But little has yet been said about their modeling of adult characteristics, though we should expect early borns to be more concerned with adults than with their less powerful siblings.

As a test of the way in which children perceive the familial situation, Houston studied boys in the two-child family by using the Bene-Anthony Family Relations Test (1957) (Sutton-Smith, Rosenberg, & Houston, 1968). This is a test in which the child sorts cards containing positive and negative statements — such as "This is someone who likes me," ". . . who plays with me," ". . . who scolds me" — into mailboxes picturing members of his family. In this exercise firstborns significantly more often sorted both positive and negative cards into the parent boxes (fathers got mainly positive mail, mothers got negative), and the later borns more often sorted the cards into the boxes of their older siblings.

These data support the view that early borns are more concerned with adults and should, therefore, model adult characteristics. There is much evidence on a variety of characteristics that suggests that this is what is happening — none of these studies is conclusive by itself, but collectively they make sense. Thus, early borns more often take adultlike roles (Sutton-Smith, Roberts, & Rosenberg, 1964); they show a preference for organizing the behavior of others; they are more dominant and more conservative, have more conscience, and are more verbal (Sampson, 1965). Hence, what we have to reconcile for the firstborns is how they can both be dependent and seeking social comparison as in the Schachter derived studies (no one has yet shown that it is the *same* siblings who are both affiliative and conforming, a basic test of construct validity) and, at the same time, be as adultlike as these other characteristics suggest. We view their dependency as a reaction to their relationships with parents, and their adultlike characteristics both as modeling after the parents and as a part of their reaction to younger siblings; this dual character of early borns gains considerable support in the literature. Thus, when in a dependent relationship (or when the social situation is ambiguous), early borns are more concerned to discover what the group consensus is. They are more likely to choose people who are popular sociometrically (Schachter, 1964). Their friendships tend to be with those they see as more powerful than themselves (Sutton-Smith, 1966) — here their reactions may be regarded as generalized from those they have established with their parents. On the other hand, when in positions of authority — that is, when they know they represent the group consensus — early borns make a greater attempt to influence the others and to expel deviants from the group (Gordon, 1966). As teachers, firstborns have been found to be more critical, disapproving, and hostile (Solomon, 1965), but at the same time also more nurturant in a reward situation, giving out more reinforcement to others (Weiss, 1966). These behavior contradictions so remarkably parallel those observed by Hilton and mentioned earlier in the behavior of mothers with their firstborns that it is a reasonable speculation that they have been generalized from parental models.

SECOND BORNS

Whereas the reactive characteristics (dependency, affiliation, conformity) of the firstborns were clearer than their modeling characteristics, with the second borns the reverse holds. They definitely model the sex role (and perhaps the power) of their elders, but their reactive characteristics are less clear. They are in a position where they have to model both siblings and parents. The parents relate to them less frequently and probably less powerfully than they do to the early born. On the other hand, elder siblings do tend to exercise considerable, often unalleviated power over them. So instead of one class of model above (parents) and an unimportant class below (younger siblings), the later born have two classes of models of varying but powerful characteristics above them. They are, therefore, subjected to a wider variety of power communications and requirements than are the early born and are given fewer consistent and explicit (verbal) cues to how they should behave. We might expect them, therefore, to have a wider variety of reactions (or role behaviors) and to rely more often on perceptual and motor modeling than on verbal cues.

Some of the scattered evidence of their role-taking characteristics might be interpreted in this way. Stotland and Dunn's (1962) data seem to show they are more empathic with peers; they have also been shown to make better inferences based on perceptual cues, posture, and gesture (whereas early borns make better inferences based on words) (Altus, 1966; Koch, 1954; Rosenberg & Sutton-Smith, 1965). They do better in role-taking experiments (Sutton-Smith & Rosenberg, 1966; 1967). In fact, they seem to be more tolerant and flexible in a number of ways (Eisenman, 1965; Sampson, 1965; Solomon, 1965). Thus, though a certain duality of role-taking characteristics may be most notable in the early born, in the later born, their role flexibility seems the most notable.

Whether we focus on the early or later born, however, there is obviously a need for studies in which both parents and their children are subjects

148

within the same research design. We have performed such a study comparing the femininity of fathers with all daughters, all sons, or mixed siblings (Rosenberg & Sutton-Smith, 1968), and another comparing the femininity of children with fathers absent and present (Sutton-Smith & Rosenberg, 1968). Although a survey of the literature leads to talk of the duality of firstborns' roles and the flexibility of the later borns' roles, these two studies just mentioned actually involving both parents and siblings have led to some novel and surprising findings; they suggest that the available data on siblings may be much less than adequate as a guide to the constellational effects we are likely to find when total families are considered in terms of many of the variables currently of importance in the literature.

Conclusion

Across the three types of interaction dealt with here — parent-child, child-child, and constellational — the several different theoretical approaches can each claim some small segment of the data. Schachter's infant-deterministic thesis obtains support both in what parents do to infants and in the dependent characteristics of the children themselves; it finds only more restricted support in the behavior of older persons. Koch's contention that sex role typing is a key influence at the age of six seems most relevant in explaining some of the departures from the infant results. The eminence and achievement data favoring only children, then firstborns, and last middle borns have never been adequately explained, but we favor the view that the sheer quantity of interaction may subsume more specialized interpretations. Hilton's recent explanations in terms of contradictory parents and dependent offspring show considerable theoretical promise.

The child-child sex and power data seem to provide clear evidence that the older siblings have a greater effect on the younger than vice versa. In fact, the dominant impression one gets from that literature is the virtue of vicarious modeling as an explanatory principle in accounting for the behavior of the second born. The less well-documented material on later borns' empathy, role flexibility, and postural-gestural inference may be taken as a testament to the skill developed by later borns in such vicarious modeling processes.

In the sections on dependency and achievement, however, we discussed the early borns' behavior mainly in terms of their reactions to their parents

149

as opposed to modeling after them. When their modeling behavior is considered — their verbalism, conservatism, attempts to influence, and so forth — we have a dialectical picture of subjects who both conform to authority and yet seek to exercise it, which is what we might expect of their actual role position between parents and later-born siblings. More importantly, however, their modeling behavior appears often to involve what would usually be thought of as central mediating (verbal, conscience, etc.) variables rather than behavioral variables. It may therefore be no accident that identification theories have always appeared to have greater relevance for firstborns than later borns — which is to say that when the modeling of firstborns and later borns is compared, the process itself as well as the targets may be different. For each group, modeling may have a different utility and be in a different style.

The other feature of the data reviewed which deserves mention is the evidence of reactive or counteractive modeling. The firstborns' modeling of the parent who is opposite in sex to the newborn sibling, the boy with two sisters acting more masculine, the father with two daughters reporting more masculine — all are similar in that the subject models an opposite rather than the target, though it is again clear that we are here lumping together quite different contents and perhaps different processes.

Still, whatever these processes come to be named, what seems necessary is more molecular attention to the actual character of the actions and reactions occurring within the various classes of interaction. Most of our knowledge is still built up too indirectly, by inferring such processes from thrice-removed dependent variables.

References

Altus, W. D. Birth order and its sequalae. *Science*, 1966, 151, 44–49.

Bayer, A. E. Birth order and college attendance. *Journal of Marriage and Family Living*, 1966, 28, 480–484.

———, & J. K. Folger. The current state of birth order and research. *Journal of Psychiatry*, 1967, 3, 37–39.

Bene, E., & J. Anthony. *Manual for the family relations test*. London: National Foundation of Educational Research, 1957.

Bragge, B. W. E., & V. L. Allen. Ordinal position and conformity. Paper presented at the meeting of the American Psychological Association, New York, September 1966.

Brim, O. G. Family structure and sex role learning by children. A further analysis of Helen Koch's data. *Sociometry*, 1958, 21, 1–16.

Cushna, B. Agency and birth order differences in very early childhood. Paper presented at the meeting of the American Psychological Association, New York, September 1966.

Eisenman, R. Birth order, aesthetic preference and volunteering for an electric shock experiment. *Psychonomic Science*, 1965, 3, 151–152.

Gewirtz, J. L. *Succorance in young children*. Ph.D. thesis. State Univ. of Iowa, Iowa City, 1948.

Gilmore, J. B., & E. Zigler. Birth order and social reinforcer effectiveness with children. *Child Development*, 1964, 35, 193–200.

Gordon, B. F. Influence and social comparison as motives for affiliation, in B. Latane, ed., *Studies in social comparison*, pp. 55–65. *Journal of Experimental Social Psychology*, 1966, Suppl. 1.

Harris, I. *The promised seed: A comparative study of first and later sons*. Glencoe, Ill.: Free Press, 1964.

Hilton, I. Differences in the behavior of mothers towards first and later born children. *Journal of Personality and Social Psychology*, 1967, 7, 282–290.

———. The dependent first born and how he grew, in B. G. Rosenberg (Chm.), Ordinal position, personality, and social interaction within the family. Symposium presented at the meeting of the American Psychological Association, San Francisco, September 1968.

Jones, H. E. Order of birth in relation to the development of the child, in C. Murchison, ed., *A handbook of child psychology*, pp. 204–241. Worcester, Mass.: Clark University Press, 1931.

Kammeyer, D. Birth order as a research variable. *Social Forces*, 1967, 46, 71–80.

Kemper, T. D. Mate selection and marital satisfaction according to sibling type of husband and wife. *Journal of Marriage and Family Living*, 1966, 28, 346–349.

Koch, H. L. The relation of "primary mental abilities" in five- and six-year-olds to sex of child and characteristics of his sibling. *Child Development*, 1954, 25, 209–223.

———. The relation of certain family constellation characteristics and the attitudes of children toward adults. *Child Development*, 1955, 26, 13–40.

———. Sissiness and tomboyishness in relation to sibling characteristics. *Journal of Genetic Psychology*, 1956, 88, 231–244. (a)

———. Some emotional attitudes of the young child in relation to characteristics of his sibling. *Child Development*, 1956, 27, 393–426. (b)

———. The relation of certain formal attributes of siblings to attitudes held toward each other and toward their parents. *Monographs for the Society for Research in Child Development*, 1960, 25 (4, Serial No. 78).

Lasko, J. K. Parent behavior towards first and second children. *Genetic Psychology Monographs*, 1954, 49, 97–137.

Leventhal, G. S. Sex of sibling, birth order and behavior of male college students from two child families. Unpublished ms., Department of Psychology, North Carolina State University, 1966.

Rosenberg, B. G., & B. Sutton-Smith. Ordinal position and sex role identification. *Genetic Psychology Monographs*, 1964, 70, 297–328. (a)

———. The relationship of ordinal position and sibling sex status to cognitive abilities. *Psychonomic Science*, 1964, 1, 81–82. (b)

———. Sibling differences in empathic style. *Perceptual and Motor Skills*, 1965, 21, 811–814.

———. Sibling association, family size, and cognitive abilities. *Journal of Genetic Psychology*, 1966, 109, 271–279.

———. Family interaction effects on masculinity-femininity. *Journal of Personality and Social Psychology*, 1968, 8, 117–120.

———. Sibling age spacing effects upon cognition. *Developmental Psychology*, in press.

Sampson, E. E. The study of ordinal position: Antecedents and outcomes, in B.

151

Maher, ed., *Progress in experimental personality research*, Vol. II, pp. 175–228. New York: Academic Press, 1965.

──────, & F. T. Hancock. Ordinal position, socialization, personality development, and conformity. *Journal of Personality and Social Psychology*, 1967, 5, 398–407.

Schachter, S. *The psychology of affiliation*. Stanford, Calif.: Stanford University Press, 1959.

──────. Birth order and sociometric choice. *Journal of Abnormal Social Psychology*, 1964, 68, 453–456.

Schoonover, S. M. The relationship of intelligence and achievement to birth order, sex of sibling, and age interval. *Journal of Educational Psychology*, 1959, 50, 143–146.

Solomon, D. Birth order, family composition and teaching style. *Psychological Reports*, 1965, 17, 871–874.

Stotland, E., & R. E. Dunn. Identification, "oppositeness," authoritarianism, self-esteem and birth order. *Psychological Monographs*, 1962, 76 (9, Whole No. 528).

Sutton-Smith, B. Play preference and play behavior: A validity study. *Psychological Reports*, 1965, 16, 65–66.

──────. Role replication and reversal in play. *Merrill-Palmer Quarterly*, 1966, 12, 285–298.

──────. Sibling differences in terms of patterns of family interaction, in B. G. Rosenberg (Chm.), Ordinal position, personality, and social interaction within the family. Symposium presented at the meeting of the American Psychological Association, San Francisco, September 1968.

──────, J. M. Roberts, & B. G. Rosenberg. Sibling associations and role involvements. *Merrill-Palmer Quarterly*, 1964, 10, 25–38.

Sutton-Smith, B., & B. G. Rosenberg. Age changes in the effects of ordinal position or sex role identification. *Journal of Genetic Psychology*, 1965, 107, 61–73.

──────. The dramatic sibling. *Perceptual and Motor Skills*, 1966, 22, 993–994.

──────. The dramatic boy. *Perceptual and Motor Skills*, 1967, 25, 247–248.

──────. Sibling consensus on power tactics. *Journal of Genetic Psychology*, 1968, 112, 63–72.

──────. *The sibling*. New York: Holt, in press.

Sutton-Smith, B., B. G. Rosenberg, & S. Houston. Sibling perception of family models. Paper presented at the meeting of the Eastern Psychological Association, Washington, D.C., 1968.

────── & F. Landy. Father absence effects in families of different sibling composition. *Child Development*, 1968, 39, 1213–1221.

Walters, R. H., & E. Ray. Anxiety, isolation, and reinforcer effectiveness. *Journal of Personality*, 1960, 28, 358–367.

Weiss, R. L. Acquiescence response set and birth order. *Journal of Consulting Psychology*, 1966, 30, 365.

LIST OF CONTRIBUTORS

List of Contributors

GORDON N. CANTOR received his Ph.D. from the Institute of Child Behavior and Development (known at the time as the Iowa Child Welfare Research Station) of the University of Iowa in 1954. He was a faculty member in the Department of Psychology at George Peabody College for Teachers from 1954 to 1960. In 1960, he returned to the University of Iowa, where he is now Assistant Director of the Institute of Child Behavior and Development and Professor of Child Psychology.

VICTOR H. DENENBERG is Professor of Behavioral Sciences and Psychology at the University of Connecticut. He received his Ph.D. at Purdue University in 1953, spent two years with Human Resources Research Office at Fort Knox, Kentucky, and then returned to Purdue University, where he initiated his research activities concerning early experiences. He moved to the University of Connecticut in 1969.

WENDELL E. JEFFREY received his Ph.D. from the University of Iowa in 1951. After four years as an Assistant Professor of Psychology at Barnard College, Columbia University, he moved to UCLA, where he is now Professor of Psychology and Director of the Developmental Psychology Training Program. His research has focused on various aspects of the development of discriminal processes in infancy and early childhood.

ELEANOR E. MACCOBY is Professor of Psychology at Stanford University. She earned her Ph.D. at the University of Michigan in 1950, and was a lecturer in the Department of Social Relations at Harvard, and a research associate in the Laboratory of Human Development there, before going to Stanford in 1958. She currently is embarked on a longitudinal study of the development of social attachment in infancy.

MUZAFER SHERIF is currently Professor of Social Psychology at the Pennsylvania State University, whose faculty he joined in 1966 after sixteen years at the University of Oklahoma as Research Professor and Director of the Institute of Group Relations. Recipient of the American Psychological Association's Distinguished Scientific Contribution Award in 1968 and the Kurt Lewin Memorial Award in 1967, he is continuing the research program reported in this volume with further study of group solidarity and individual attitudes. CAROLYN W. SHERIF, who is collaborating in the research, is Associate Professor of Psychology at the Pennsylvania State University. The most recent of their several joint publications is a major revision of their 1956 social psychology text published in May 1969.

BRIAN SUTTON-SMITH received his Ph.D. from the University of New Zealand in 1954 and is now Principal Advisor in Developmental Psychology at Teachers College, Columbia University. His primary research interests are in social and play development. B. G. ROSENBERG received his Ph.D. from the University of California at Berkeley in 1952. He is Professor of Psychology at Bowling Green State University and has a major research interest in sex role development.

INDEX

Index

Achievement: birth order and, 133, 134–135, 146, 149

Adolescence: reference groups in, 101–104, 111, 112, 115–125, 126–128; physical growth in, 102; self-concept in, 102; adult expectations in, 102–103; influence of age-mates in, 103–104, 124–125; parental influence in, 103–104; sociocultural setting and, 105, 106–111; self-radius in, 107–111

Adrenocortical activity: nature of mother and, 41

Affective reactions: to familiarized stimuli, 24

Affiliation: birth order and, 133, 135–139, 147; social comparison theory and, 135; conformity studies of, 135–136; pain reduction and, 136–137

Aggression: measurement of, 32; nature of mother and, 32; genetic basis for, in mouse, 32, 37; spontaneity of, in mouse, 32, 37; birth order and, 143–144

Attending responses, *see* Attention

Attention: and stimulus familiarization, 15, 80–81; in early experience studies, 48; visual, 48–65, 68–69, 70, 71–73, 73–74, 79, 83, 85–86, 89, 91; motion parallax and, 49, 55, 56; movement of stimulus in, 50; in problem-solving, 50, 61, 62; reinforcement and, 50, 72–73; to interface between object and surround, 55; context and, 55, 89–93; novelty-induced conflict and, 56; domination of by color and brightness, 57; in darkness, 59; language and, 62, 89; as central event, 64, 68, 69, 73–74, 77–78, 78–81; potential

stimulation and, 68; receptor orientation and, 68, 69, 70–73, 74, 77, 88; significance of stimulus and, 68, 70, 72; to informative features, 68, 70, 72, 78, 88; contour-tracing and, 68, 70–71, 72; and attenuation of impulse amplitude, 68–69; memory and, 69, 73–74, 82, 84–86, 87–88, 92–93; auditory, 69, 74–78, 79–83, 83–85, 86–89, 91; tactual, 70, 71; distinctive features and, 70, 72; task-set and, 70–73, 73–74, 77–78, 81–94; methodology in study of, 71, 73–74, 75; stimulus complexity and, 72, 89; dichotic listening studies of, 74–75, 76, 77, 81–82, 83–94; response factors in, 75–76, 86–87; peripheral masking and, 76; discrimination learning and, 78, 81, 88–89; filter theory of, 78–81, 93; and preattentive processes, 79, 93; discriminability and, 80–81, 92; divided, 81–94; sequential probability of phrases and, 87–88; centering and, 90; incidental learning and, 91. *See also* Orienting responses; Stimulus familiarization

– development of: control by external stimulus in, 50–51, 52, 53; in infancy, 50–65; habituation and, 51–52, 53–54, 58; maturation in, 53; model for, 53; acceleration of scanning in, 56; in passive organism, 58–59; receptor orientation in, 70–73; to informative material, 70–73; to wanted stimulus from complex array, 73–76; selective sets and, 77–94; discrimination learning and, 81; divided, 81–94; to complex stimulus, 82–84; memory trace in, 84–86; response inter-

159

INDEX

Stress: and physical growth, 35–36, 39; and menarche, 36, 39; infant handling and, 41

Timidity: infant stimulation and, 39

Transfer: in learning, 49

Urbanization: index of, 105

Welsh Figure Preference Test: 17, 18, 21, 24

Weight: infant handling and, 41; nature of mother and, 41